I0815416

storied style
The Book about You, your story, and how to design your Home with it
GRACE MITCHELL
HARPER HORIZON

To Ellis, Tate, GloryEvelyn, and Karis,
the best part of my story,
and to Kent, my love,
who inspired me with the idea of "storied style" in the first place.

And also, for the misfits and the dreamers,
and anyone who has ever put themselves out there
(or is still just thinking about it).

from your friend, grace

STORIED STYLE

Published by Harper Horizon, an imprint of HarperCollins Focus LLC, 501 Nelson Place, Nashville, TN 37214, USA.

ISBN 978-1-4002-5308-1 (HC)
ISBN 978-1-4002-5309-8 (ePub)

HarperCollins Publishers, Macken House, 39/40 Mayor Street Upper, Dublin 1, D01 C9W8, Ireland (https://www.harpercollins.com)

Library of Congress Control Number: 2025938475

Art director: Belinda Bass and Darren Holdway
Cover and interior design: Darren Holdway

Printed in Italy

25 26 27 28 29 RTL 5 4 3 2 1

~~CONTENTS~~

Here's How It's Gonna Go, y'all

What If?!

What if I told you I love "what if" questions? There's such hopefulness and excitement in them—just what I want to convey when it comes to putting together a home you'll love.

When I was a child, Creativity was my comrade and Imagination my friend. I spent hours making things for my dollhouse—stitching tissues together for quilts and pillows (my dad would often joke he should buy stock in Kleenex and Scotch tape), monogramming tiny napkins, and making furniture from nature finds in my backyard. And when I wasn't crafting little worlds with my hands, I was creating them in my head. I was consistently writing some story; and if not writing, then constantly reading—voraciously! There were times I would check out three books from the school library and return them the next day for three more. Our school librarian, Mrs. Claunch, whom I adored, would chuckle at me, her good-humored eyes crinkling behind her large clear-framed glasses, and shake her head in amusement.

You might guess a kid so wrapped up in her own imagination got bullied a little. But you'd be wrong—I was bullied a lot. Looking back, I'm not exactly sure what made me the target, but I was always just . . . different. I didn't dress like the other kids, I didn't act like them, and I was awkward. Picture me: very tall, very thin, with a large head (eventually with lots of wild, curly hair) perched on a tiny neck. When we walked as a class in a line, I did not like to see over everyone else's head—or for everyone else to see mine popping up out of the midst—so I would walk with my knees bent, hiding my beanpole legs under my long skirt. I got braces in second grade and did not get them off until almost my junior year of high school. "Brace Face Grace" was my nickname (BFG for short), and no, it was not a term of endearment. I remember trying to smile with my mouth closed—which I couldn't accomplish because of some very advanced buck teeth. I remember trying to think of topics to talk about that were still in my comfort zone to make me more palatable. I remember dreading picture day, presentation day, or any day when we had to pick partners.

Recently I was telling my youngest daughter (rather cringingly) how in eighth grade I would listen to the Top 40 on my brother's world band radio underneath my pillow while falling asleep every night so I could use the music as a talking point at school, hoping to spark friendship. But my attempts to be included invariably seemed to fall short. Even though I didn't want to be looked at, I still wanted to be seen. *Please, someone just sit by me at lunch today,* I'd pray. Yet they never did. Instead, most days of seventh grade the same group of girls would find me at PE, encircle me, and dump me in the big trash can behind the school.

To be sure, my diaries from these years (one with Strawberry Shortcake and one with pink hearts) had their share of silly, happy recollections, but there

you're the biggest dork that ever dorked

I told everyone not to sign your yearbook

you drew like my grandma

hey metal mouth!

Brace Face Grace has a gross face

only nerds read as many books as you

no one likes you

you are so ugly, no one will ever want to marry you

I'm asking everyone to my birthday party except you

no one wants to be friends with you

were a lot of sad things, even hurtful things, I told myself. I simply could not understand why people treated me the way they did. The world was broken in some way I could not fix, could not set right. Still, sprinkled here and there was something else: stories of hope. All I could do was manage my own little part, the piece I could control, and give the thing that seemed to be in such short supply: kindness. I could be kind to people. Maybe because of the stories I immersed myself in, I could imagine people acting out because of something going on in their lives I did not know about.

Now that I'm older, I find that early instinct to be largely true. Of course, if I could go back, I would have better tools to stand up for myself. But all those years of ridicule bloomed into something really beautiful in me—a listening ear and eyes to see the people around me.

In fifth grade, I had my first real best friend. She gifted me with one of my most sentimental possessions, something I passed on to my two girls: a beautiful hardcover copy of *Anne of Green Gables* by L. M. Montgomery. It's the story of a young orphan girl named Anne with a big imagination. She has a rather dreadful life before being adopted by a brother and sister in their fifties who live in a house they call Green Gables on Canada's Prince Edward Island. As much as I loved books—and I had some real favorites by then—nothing had ever captured my heart like "Anne with an e" (because the character insists she could never be a plain *A-n-n*). Montgomery's depiction of Anne in all her stages ignited my creativity and spoke to my soul. Reading Anne's innermost thoughts was like looking in a mirror. The way she saw the world—her optimistic point of view, her hopefulness in the face of crushing circumstances, her delight in the simple beauty of nature, her intricate descriptions of people and how she interpreted their responses to life's scenarios—these things resonated with me in a way I do not believe I have ever experienced again. Her ability to face life's struggles and hardships with resilience and a positive outlook, instead of ignoring them, greatly influenced my life.

Not too long ago I spotted my treasured copy of *Anne of Green Gables* on the table in our living room, as my daughter had been reading it. I picked it up just to see where she was, but once I had it in my hands, I couldn't help but hunt for a few of my favorite passages. Here's one I've always loved: "There's such a lot of different Annes in me. I sometimes think that is why I'm such a troublesome person. If I was just the one Anne it would be ever so much more comfortable, but then it wouldn't be half so interesting."

Of course, after a quick flip through, I promptly turned to the first page and read the whole story from beginning to end in one night—laughing, remembering, and, yes, shedding a tear or twenty. Reading the words that penetrated my heart all those years ago made adult me sit and reflect. As we age, we go through hardships and heartaches; the difficulties of life leave scars, writing out whole chapters of hurt. Some pages are for friends, others for family, and some are ours alone. It is easy to lose sight of hope, to lose the magic of dreaming, to miss the importance of imagination, when walking through real life.

You may be wondering why I am telling you this. I promise I have a point! Creating a home requires a special kind of problem-solving, even a little playful scheming. Tapping into that certain childhood magic. Dare we dream, dare we imagine, dare we write a story? *Anne of Green Gables* was published in 1908, more than a century ago, and although Anne's ideas resonate differently as we grow older, her worldview seems as significant for me now as it has ever been. Maybe the context has morphed, but the truth has not. Seeing ourselves and the people around us as parts of the same story, woven and working together for the benefit of everyone—sharing pain but also purpose, sharing hope and happiness and love, sharing ourselves—this is the heart of what it means to say *home*. And I think Anne would agree, so I hope you won't mind that, over the course of this book, a few of her quotes pop up here and there.

Some people go through life trying to find out what the world holds for them only to find out too late that it's what they bring to the world that really counts.

—L. M. Montgomery, journal entry

Anne
of Green Gables
Anne
of Green
Gables
L.M.
MONTGOMERY
Illustrated by
JODY LEE
ILLUSTRATED
JUNIOR LIBRARY
GROSSET
ISBN 0-448-06030-2

story + style

When I was first breaking into the design world, I had four very young kids, limited funds, and a beat-up minivan my dad lovingly dubbed the "War Wagon." Together, the kids and I drove all over North Texas scoping out yard sales and estate sales and picking up furniture I bought off Craigslist. Estate sales were a little tricky with children; larger houses were easier to manage with my quadruple stroller, which we called "Mitchell Stadium"—two kids on top facing me and two kids on the bottom facing out. In tighter homes I would put on my double carrier, with one of my girls bound to my stomach and one to my back, while each arm scooped up one boy. We were quite the sight! I would buy homewares and furniture, list them for sale online, and often sell them before I even pulled back into my driveway! It was a nice little side hustle.

My husband was working long, long hours in those years, too, doing quite a bit of hustling himself to get through his school program and working extra jobs to provide for our young family. As is true for a lot of young couples, having children had not been an easy road for us. We'd had three miscarriages at ten to twelve weeks and then lost a baby boy five months into the pregnancy. If this is something you have been through, my heart goes out to you. It is a lonely grief, and there are many deeply felt aspects to it—physical, emotional, and spiritual. Walking through that experience gave me a gratitude for my children from day one I would not have had otherwise—even when I was feeling a little overwhelmed upon finding out I was four months pregnant with number two when number one was only six months old! My whole life I'd dreamed of being a mom, so although it was a pretty crazy time, I was overjoyed to have a full vehicle with four car seats and four children ages three and under (nope, no multiples)!

Granny and Papa Zack

Barbie Kleenex Quilt

9th Grade

Old Home Supply

The farm

How we laid out our new house

Forever a Clampett

Seaside, a fave destination

Backyard Living

At some point most new moms still feel like kids themselves, and I was no different. I distinctly remember looking at my four blond babies and wondering, *Who in the world let me have all of these kids? Am I really qualified for this?* It did not seem all that long ago I was in elementary school making a valentine box for the art contest, writing fairy stories, and bartering for craft supplies.

When I was seventeen, I filled out the "share your interests" questionnaire at the beginning of my PSAT. At first I stared blankly at the list of college majors I was supposed to choose from. Then I read the words *Interior Design*, and something sparked. I filled in the bubble. By this point I had grown into myself a bit. No longer was I ostracized; I had settled into a fun social life. I like to joke that I grew into my face. The

ABOVE Wallpaper adds a fun element to the stairs. It held up well because we brushed it with a matte clear sealant. **LEFT** The side entry of our old home accented with picture rail molding.

braces were gone, my frizzy hair had relaxed, and my proportions looked a little more natural, if you will.

Interior design was my initial major in college, until I met with an adviser who told me it was a dying field, and I should use my brain for something more useful. I had probably eight different majors after that (I'm a girl with many interests), but an American Sign Language (ASL) class I took to fulfill my foreign language credit completely changed my path. ASL is a beautiful, expressive language, and I loved it. I was a dancer growing up, and practicing ASL was like dancing with words. It's a more difficult language to learn than you might think, with its own system of grammar (it's not simply signed English), but I immersed myself in it, signing in my head to songs, to commercials, and in conversation. My degree track, a bachelor of science, focused on different modalities in instructing the Deaf, but I decided I wanted to initially pursue teaching. In my senior year of college, a car accident that nearly took my life postponed my ability to graduate. A long stay in the hospital and an extended recovery delayed my post-college life, but I made it through, accepting my degree a year later.

After graduating, I started my career as a teacher for Deaf and Hard-of-Hearing middle schoolers in the public school system, and I eventually obtained a master's degree in educational philosophy. After finishing my graduate program, I became a language therapist for Deaf and Hard-of-Hearing babies ages newborn through three. It was then I met Kent, my future husband. We married, and before we needed car seats, we were able to participate in medical mission work for Deaf communities across the world. Since ASL is a universal language, you can use it anywhere in the world to communicate with the Deaf. It was a rich time of seeing places I had previously only read about in books. My eyes were opened to different ways of living and the many paths of life. Getting to see how families operated across the globe, being welcomed into different types of homes, and realizing the beauty of creating a family culture spurred me on to dream of having my own family.

After our miscarriages, I decided to pursue my doctorate in audiology, thinking that throwing myself into school would help me cope with my grief. We were surprised a short time later to find out we were pregnant again, with our first son, Ellis. The rest of our kiddos (Tate, GloryEvelyn, and Karis) came a little

ABOVE I like for each kid to have a labeled cup near a water station. It saves your countertop from a cluttering of one-use glasses!
RIGHT It's my goal to use every square inch of space in a kitchen. A shallow, narrow cabinet inset between studs holds batteries, boo-boo supplies, tools, and other household essentials.

faster than we'd planned, though we welcomed them all with gusto, and a few years later I found myself at home in a bustling cottage full of babies.

For the first time in many years, I was at home *a lot*. And I poured myself into making it happy. Raising a young family was exhausting at times, but it also gave me a renewed energy to create, to make, to dream. I immersed myself in the fashioning of young imaginations: dumping flour on the kitchen floor to write letters in; going to the farmers' market or fancy grocery store to look at all the colors, shapes, and textures of fruits and veggies; making paints from flowers; documenting our long walks with homemade books and collected leaves and rocks. I've always been a morning person *and* a night owl. I loved working at night, with no interruptions, when the house was quiet and still—painting a room, devouring design books, teaching myself to sew. I could feel bubbling back to the surface that little girl who relished making miniature *Better Homes & Gardens* magazines for her Barbie house and delighted in fashioning tiny room-design dioramas. (I guess my life came full-circle when, years later, my own home—the human-sized one—was featured in *BHG*.)

I first heard the word *blog* back when I was in graduate school, and I distinctly remember thinking, *Why would anyone ever want to read things I wrote about my life?* But after my husband gifted me a portfolio inscribed with "Show others your Storied Style," my website was born.

The transition was a little scary. I went from making decent money flipping furniture to sitting up late into the night writing—for free. But slowly (very slowly) my website and design ideas began to get noticed. I gained followers; I got comments; I started to land brand deals, in which I got to try out and style new products for my (gasp) audience. These opportunities opened the door to magazines—physical publications I could touch and hold, a different form of writing, and a whole new world of photo shoots and styling I quickly came to love. Being a detail-oriented person, I found the process of setting up and formatting beautiful photos endlessly fascinating. It was something I could really get into. In those early days, I would offer to tag along as an unpaid assistant on any shoot I heard about just so I could learn.

Back on the home front, my abode was my design lab—I was constantly tweaking and experimenting,

ABOVE LEFT Because this was a rather narrow kitchen, I thought lights hanging over the island would be a distraction. Flushmount lights geometrically arranged in a series keep the eye moving. **ABOVE RIGHT** That $100 salvaged window brought so much light into this kitchen. **RIGHT** This was an original sink in our old 1919 home! We plumbed a filter and a chiller in the cabinet underneath the water station.

1 2 3 4

"I'd like to add some beauty to life," said Anne dreamily. "I don't exactly want to make people *know* more... though I know that *is* the noblest ambition... but I'd love to make them have a pleasanter time because of me... to have some little joy or happy thought that would never have existed if I hadn't been born."

—L.M. Montgomery,
Anne of Avonlea

putting my background in science to good use. I will say, it was not the easiest or the most comfortable period, especially for my husband. He would come home, and the sofa—or the bed—would be missing. Sometimes I would have replaced the missing object already because I found something amazing secondhand; sometimes I simply felt it was time for a change. We even had a mattress on the floor for a few years during the quest for the perfect bed. (We were Scandinavian chic before it was cool!) Yes, whatever part of our home I was photographing looked amazing, but the rest of the house? Well, let's just say it was ~~piles of mess~~ a work in progress.

At any rate, my portfolio grew, and people liked what I had done with my home and wanted me to help them with theirs. This was all very exciting to me, and though I had big dreams, I did not make clear goals. I worried if I clung too closely to timelines and bullet points, I might miss the opportunity right in front of me: enjoying and investing in my young family. I didn't want to let one moment go by without really living it. I knew this time of my life was fleeting, a blip. So each little success, each new mention, each unexpected phone call—they were all just pleasant surprises.

The kids got a little older, the quadruple stroller went to storage, my work gained a larger audience, and I had a little more time to take on clients. But because I did not have a formal education in interior design (after all, that was only one of my many discarded majors), I hesitated to call myself a designer. I felt I still had so much to learn, and I was hungry to learn all I could. So I got to work creating my own curriculum, poring over books about design and trailblazing artists and style makers. Researching what respected universities used for their interior design programs, I soaked in books about pattern and furniture history, along with designer biographies, piecing together a library of people who really shook up the design world: Edith Wharton, Elsie de Wolfe, Dorothy Draper, and many others. I took particular interest in how modern-day designers were building on the ideas of the past.

Home tours were something my parents enjoyed, so as a child I had gone on several, to old historic homes and new builds alike. I loved them, especially the older houses. Now, if a noteworthy home is available to tour and it's within driving distance, I am there. Even when we travel, I search for significant structures to explore. I've hauled my husband and kids into more historic homes than you can imagine. When an old house pops up for sale nearby, I will swing through just to check out the architecture and design. And if I see one that looks empty and abandoned, I'm breakin' in, ahem—calling the owner to see whether I can take a tour.

"It's not about what you want to prove but what you have to say. And I don't want my signature on your home— I want yours."

Home design and decor trends are ever changing, and though there is nothing new under the sun, the fashions of old can be rich inspiration for the current and the fresh. I've always thought this to be true, and the more I learned, the more I made this my mantra.

Around this time I got to meet someone in the design world I greatly respected. I was thrilled to talk with her (and maybe a little overzealous), and I spilled out my whole design philosophy, hoping for feedback, looking for guidance. Her response, however, was not what I wanted to hear.

You see, in my work with clients, I noticed a fairly common thread. Many of them had worked with a designer already or copied a home they liked out of a magazine, but they were unhappy. Some spent a lot of money and disliked the outcome, and it was painful to think of changing things again. They did not feel at home in their space, and many times they could not quite put their finger on why. I love the challenge of figuring out what is wrong and homing in on what the client is really wanting. Something Anne of Green Gables is really good at is peering beneath the surface, looking past the words people say and somehow seeing the heart of what they really mean. With that in mind, I started looking for a way to bypass the canned designer-ready answers and get to something a little deeper.

Most of the time, potential clients want to show me photos and online vision boards of what they like. Don't get me wrong—this is helpful, but not in the essential way people might imagine. Over the years I've discovered that our story points the way to our style more than anything else. So when a client hands me a stack of pages torn from a magazine or sends the password to a website wish list, I set those things aside, assure the client we'll get there, and start trying to learn their story. And one of the best ways of getting to know someone is by asking questions . . . and then really listening to the answers.

The solution to creating a home in which someone feels they belong is not found on popular websites or in trendy magazines; it's much more personal than that. Choices based on inspiration from others don't work and end up feeling flat. Just as people are all different, with their own kaleidoscopes of likes and interests, their homes—their most intimate spaces—should reflect these distinct and beautiful qualities.

So back to that mentor I sought advice from. What did she say that seemed so wrong? Well, creating homes around clients' stories is the exact opposite of what she told me to do. "Pick a style," she said, "and stick to it. Repeat, repeat, repeat. Make every home your signature. That's the only way you are going to survive if you want to make money at this."

This method works for many designers whose work I love. But I just couldn't do it. That road was not right for me. The memory of feeling misunderstood, unseen, even bullied, is tangible to me to this day, and my work, no matter the medium, feels more worthwhile when putting others *first*. Besides, when given the chance, I like to do things a little differently, even if that means taking a back seat. Maybe that's a funny way to forge a path, but sometimes it just feels right.

Creating *home* for others felt meaningful to me; it felt purposeful. More than a pleasing combination of pretty things, more than a space to brag about, home should be intensely personal. It's not about what you want to prove but what you have to *say*. And I don't want *my* signature on your home—*I want yours.*

KEM
K&G

A home is meant to be personal. Don't believe me? Read on.

IF YOU'RE A DOUBTER, YOU LIKELY FIT INTO ONE OF FOUR CATEGORIES. (REMEMBER, I'VE BEEN DOIN' THIS AWHILE, AND I'VE HEARD ALL OF THESE OVER AND OVER.)

1. THE "I DON'T HAVE A STORY" PERSON

A classic! You may be surprised to hear how often someone says this, unless you are this person, of course. But Mr. Rogers was right: You are special, and you have something to say and to offer the community around you. The truth is, if you are breathing, you have a story. Let's find it together through this book. Trust me, you have one, and a worthy one at that.

2. THE "BUT WHAT ABOUT RESALE?" PERSON

If you've spent any time watching a certain home television network, you might be influenced to weigh every subway-tile decision that isn't gray or white against how it could affect your home's resale value, which interferes with the infusion of you in your space. Therefore, you inhabit a house for decades paying a mortgage with the next owner in mind. Your hard-earned money is at work for someone else (that you don't even know) in the house you live in *now*. How does this make sense? You can make your home your own *and* still be wise with how you do it in case you decide to sell. But, as a rule of thumb, I do not shy away from color or personality, and we sold our last home in a matter of hours in a bidding war. Thoughtful design is good design.

3. THE "AIN'T NOBODY GOT TIME FOR THAT" PERSON

People are often too rushed, too stressed, and too busy to think about and reflect on their lives. It can feel like a waste of time, it can feel too difficult, it can be hard to pinpoint what you want to glean from your life and put into your house. I promise if you put your time into thoughtfully answering the questions I provide, you will develop a well-rounded plan for how to put your home together.

4. THE "I'LL JUST COPY AND PASTE IT" PERSON

If I had a dollar for every time a client reached out because they copied a design they liked and now hate how it turned out, I would have my feet up in a renovated chalet in France right now. We live in a world of fast-paced design. Trends change as fast as you can finish implementing them. Have you ever looked at web images or social media and thought, *Everything looks the same?* Me too! Let's bring personality back into spaces!

If you want a home that is beautiful and functional, uniquely yours, and one you will not want to change in five minutes, keep reading.

RIGHT The kitchen in the Round Top project designed by Leanne Ford and me is truly the heart of this home. The giant antique round table, vintage chairs, reclaimed lighting, and an original stained glass window create a lived-in, come-in-and-stay-awhile atmosphere.

There is perhaps nothing quite as Southern as having people over and offering them a tour the moment they step through the door. And, let's face it, people love it. We are all intrinsically nosy (some of us more than others). We want to see how our friends and acquaintances live. We want to see how they operate, how they keep things. Throwing your door open and saying, "Hey, this is my home, my story, here I am!" is a beautiful way to live—heart open, unashamed of who you are. That is *so freeing* for people, and much more meaningful than "Look at all of these pretty things I like."

I'm going to make a bold statement. You will never love your home the way you want to if you . . .

- sell yourself (and your story) short,
- design for resale, or
- rush the process.

Can gathering inspiration photos help steer you toward what you like? Yes, indeed. I would recommend looking through old design books, vintage magazines, and the web for a broad overview of what you're drawn to. But don't begin there—designing your home is a personal process, and what it really needs to shine is . . . you!

So let's get started.

"I wonder if it will be—can be—any more beautiful than this," murmured Anne, looking around her with the loving, enraptured eyes of those to whom "home" must always be the loveliest spot in the world, no matter what fairer lands may lie under alien stars.

—L.M. Montgomery, *Anne of the Island*

RIGHT The quiet elegance of this country bathroom is highlighted by the addition of the leaded windows we moved from the bedroom. The reclaimed marble vanity is a gorgeous focal point right when you walk in. (Design by myself and Leanne Ford.)

START

Tell me what you want, what you really, really want.

WITH

But don't start with photos.

DESCRIPTORS

Start by making a list of three to five adjectives that describe how you want each space to feel.

Options, options, options—they are endless when it comes to decorating your house. Mixing styles and looks can feel overwhelming. Where to begin? I promise you—it is not the internet. Instead, I have clients make me a short list of how they want their house to feel. So when I am weighing an option, I hold it up against the list. Does it fit? If not, next option. This is a tried-and-true method to help you gain confidence in your choices.

For example, if you tell me you want an *organic*, *garden-feel*, *natural* home, those adjectives make it easy to throw out the super modern wallpaper. Now, that does not mean everything in the room has to echo those characteristics precisely; it simply means the main design elements in the space reflect your desired attributes. Rooms that flow well and look collected over time almost always have elements of different styles; in fact, this is preferred. Centering your main pieces around your attributes ensures you get the look and feel you dream of and helps you narrow your focus.

It's easy to get distracted by all the possibilities. Get to whittling!

"It's lovely to be going home and know it's home."

—L. M. Montgomery, *Anne of Green Gables*

THE ARMSTRONG FAMILY TOLD ME THEY WANTED THEIR HOME TO HAVE THESE QUALITIES:

- Southern (especially New Orleans–style)
- classic/traditional
- inviting
- warm
- elegant

So I got right to work researching elements of classic Louisiana homes. Brick floors, elements of French influence, and even the classic fleur-de-lis made an appearance in the kitchen tile.

RIGHT: An open Dutch door, hydrangeas, and dentil molding—quintessentially Southern elements—invite you right in.
30–31 A clean white kitchen with French-blue accents makes for a welcoming space.
32–33 This lacquered dining room, complete with rewired vintage French lanterns made into sconces, feels refined but not stuffy. A piece of hand-painted Gracie wallpaper framed with molding is a lovely focal point. This couple's fondness for Southern style comes from their Louisiana and Mississippi family heritage. I had a local artist, Kristi Easterly, paint their beloved family homes in honor of these memories.
34–35 When the homeowner, who is a chef, showed me her collection of menus that were meaningful to her, I knew we needed to do something special with them. Turning them into wallpaper got them out of a drawer and into her home office, where they can inspire her as she plans out her seasonal menus for her restaurant.

GROW COOK EAT
On Pleasant Cooking

everybody eats there
Jacques
Shreveport's
Only
Premier Night Club
Featuring The Finest In
Live Entertainment
Jacques
Restaurant
Sheraton
Pierremont Hotel
Phone 797-9900
Imperial
Cathay
ANGELUNA
VONG
NAPA
CULINARIA Italy

THE LEE FAMILY HAD A READY ANSWER WHEN I ASKED THEM THE CHARACTERISTICS THEY WANTED THEIR HOME TO EXUDE . . .

- organic
- nature-filled with a touch of red
- musical

RIGHT The entry to this home tells you exactly how this space will feel—organic and fresh. Framing the wallpaper on the ceiling and then having it wash down the wall is a great way to use pattern without having to overly commit. Then, if you ever want to change it, it's not such an ordeal.
38–39, 42 The mix of greens in the kitchen between the dark green cabinetry and the lighter green wicker counter stools further enhances the outdoor scheme. Glass shelves installed across the windows allow the light to illuminate the dishes. Salvaged greenhouse lights over the island further the outside-come-inside feel.
40–41 The mother in this family loves the outdoors and planting, but her busy schedule with work and family does not allow much time for it. I wanted to bring the garden to her in the kitchen.
43 This is a very musical family! Instruments are displayed in the living room, ready for whenever the opportunity arises.
44 Some extra wallpaper we had was applied to the backs of the pantry doors as a fun surprise. Details delight!
45 As someone who spends serious time in the laundry room, I like to bring a happy flair to this space. The Lees got their red accent through the tile detail and wallpaper here, the botanical motif tying in the garden feel.

THE MCGUIRES PURCHASED AN OLD HOME IN NEED OF A BIG RENOVATION TO SUIT THEIR NEEDS FOR A FAMILY OF SIX. I HAPPEN TO KNOW A THING OR TWO ABOUT PRACTICAL HOMES FOR LARGE FAMILIES, SO I WAS THRILLED TO START. THEIR PREFERRED CHARACTERISTICS WERE . . .

- historic
- well-traveled
- light-filled
- comfortable
- unique

Although descriptors are a helpful tool to get you started on design plans, they are not the full extent of incorporating yourself into your home design. This practice is just the first chapter, if you will. Next, your unique story elements come into play, the main factors to develop your home's scheme. The homes I just showed you started with adjectives, yes, but adding in all the detailed story elements is what really makes those places special.

RIGHT An entry space as special as this deserved a special wall treatment. Treillage (pronounced *tray-audge*) is an intricate use of millwork derived from the French garden architecture used at Versailles. A trusted local fabricator, Joe Mello, made this vision come to life.

48 The original Batchelder fireplace was restored to remain the focal point of this living room.

49 A look into the living room from the treillage-walled entry.

50–51 The mother in this family is from Argentina, and the family loves to visit and spend plentiful time there. Tying in the color and spirit of Argentina was important to them. The pendant lights were made by an Argentinian family, and the tile represents what you would see in Buenos Aires.

52 Much thought and care went into ensuring this kitchen felt true to the heart of this home. When you do any renovation in a historic house, you want visitors to be guessing what is original and what is not. It shouldn't be blatantly obvious. I found this pair of discarded windows, original to the house, in the basement, and they became the cabinet fronts on one wall of kitchen cabinetry.

53 Peeking into the dining area, you can see the stair risers have been tiled to give a European feel.

54 Vintage maps line the walls of a little hallway, and an old door conceals a special collection of spirits.

55–57 A historic tile pattern complements the floor of the mudroom and includes the words *vida feliz*—happy life. There's lots of storage and a locker for each child, numbered *uno* through *cuatro*. Narrow drawers are labeled to hold schoolwork and art projects for each young creator.

MAISON

MAP OF THE STATE OF CALIFORNIA
BRITTON & REY
TEXAS

da feliz

UNO
DOS
TRES
CUATRO

THE SEVEN QUESTIONS

"I wonder what part of my story you would put in my home" is a fairly common statement I hear, especially from folks who watch my television show—a facet of my life that came about quite unexpectedly.

Of course, as a lover of design and home transformation, HGTV had been a favorite network of mine since college, on through my single years, and into my marriage. Having a show sounded fun and was something my husband and I would joke about, but it also seemed totally unrealistic. When I first got the call about the possibility, I was excited, but I shrugged it off as a pipe dream. And honestly, at that point, I was way out of the television loop: Too much was happening with my young family and a blooming design career. We didn't even own a TV! Much to my surprise, the pitch tape the production company sent to the network (a simple little spliced-together web interview) made it through to the next round. Then came a sizzle reel, and shortly after we got the news we were to film a pilot episode.

Back then, everyone in the running to get a television series aired a pilot episode to see how it rated, and if it did well, you were in. To my complete shock, our show made network history by being the first show to go to series without airing a pilot.

The next several months were fast and furious. A little less than halfway through our first season—and as the number one new series on HGTV—we found out we were headed for season two! Despite some early trepidation over my unique approach to design, with a few executives wondering if I was too "out there" for prime time, we found an audience—an audience excited to see something a little different every week. I will forever be grateful to my beloved Mr. Rick, Mr. Craig, Ms. Becky, and Mr. Cory—they did the work when cameras were on and off—and all the other people who believed in us, worked on those projects, and made the show happen.

The series was a hit, and people loved it. Well, not everyone, but that's okay. As my dear friend the talented artist Leanne Ford says, "If you're not doing something that makes people nervous, you're not doing anything special." This is a sentiment I wholeheartedly believe.

My inbox flooded the night our show aired, and it has not stopped. Most of what people write is kind and encouraging, but some messages are pretty miserable—something you have to get used to when you put yourself out there on such a grand scale. Though it does make me chuckle a bit to read some scathing opinion about how *they* would *hate* what I did, and they *cannot believe* I would paint cabinets blue or make a light out of a canoe or a canary cage, it can be frustrating. Clearly, these folks missed the whole point of my work. I operate in full vision of the homeowners. What I would do for one person, I would not do for another. If you tell me you do not like green, your walls will not be green.

Much of the correspondence I receive—from all over the world—is from people who want to put their stories in their homes but aren't sure how. I hope you find this book to be a complete guide for answering that question. It all begins with a little digging into yourself—putting aside any preconceived notions about how your house should look, what you are "supposed to" like and be drawn to, and what expectations you think others will have of your space. It's okay to see some of the photos in this book and think, *I would never do that in my house*. In fact, I welcome that! Being able to pinpoint what feels like home to you (and what doesn't), what makes you excited when you walk through a door, is good and beneficial. We are all different, and our residences should be too. There are things in other people's houses I would not necessarily prefer in my own home, but I can appreciate the individuality of them. There's always something to learn, always someone to be inspired by!

The foundation for my projects is a questionnaire. Over the years, my thought process and list of questions have become much more efficient. It makes me laugh to look back at the rather extensive document I made my early clients fill out. Sorry, y'all! Thankfully, I've narrowed down the list of queries that crack the code: what's interesting, what's notable, what's worthy of display. My enthusiasm in writing this book is in equipping you with my exact process—so you can start telling your own story in your home and maybe even rediscover yourself a little along the way.

"Everything that's worth having is some trouble."

—L. M. Montgomery, *Anne of Avonlea*

As I've put together my own home five different times, plus many clients' homes, I've come up with seven central questions for designing a house around the homeowner's story. Using this framework as a guide is a great way to get a style that is beautiful, comfortable, and uniquely you. Of course, you need not apply the answers to every space. Perhaps you'll spread them out into various rooms or focus mainly on one answer in one special area. It's up to you. One of the most appealing aspects of using your story to fuel the design of your home is it enables you to have a rich, personalized home at any price point. It's not about a certain style or look or brand; it's about you, your family, your people, your one special life.

In a world of constantly changing trends (who can even keep up?!), using these questions ensures your rooms will not look the same as a million others you see all over social media. And just so you know, it's okay if you don't immediately have a response to a question. This is a practice in self-reflection and patience. No home is put together in a day. In fact, it's best if it is not. Allow yourself the freedom of slowing your mind and exploring your thoughts and memories. I recommend keeping a journal with your responses, or maybe even emailing yourself to collect your thoughts in one place.

We live in a busy society where it feels hard to decelerate, especially if we're slowing down just to think. But taking time to review the past, to consider what is meaningful to us, is a task worth doing (and very often overlooked). It's not the quick way, though. And it's not the easy way either. Just picking something pretty feels a lot simpler, doesn't it? But I believe hasty decisions do not stand the test of time. It's the ones we marinate on that seem to make the most impact. Our fast-paced world has trained us not to do this. It feels too cumbersome, too hard, like a waste of time. We want things done yesterday at the latest. But when you pace yourself while putting together your home, you actually save time (since you don't have to redo all the things you discover you don't really like or can't live with). And besides having a space you enjoy that feels like you, you'll also save money by avoiding the expensive game of guessing what others might like several years from now if you decide to sell. All it takes is pressing pause (which, yes, I realize is a big ask) and reflecting for a while on what makes you *you*.

"I *do* know my own mind," protested Anne. "The trouble is, my mind changes and then I have to get acquainted with it all over again."

—L. M. Montgomery, *Anne of the Island*

Okay, so you're on board! You want your home to reflect you, but where to begin? As often happens, once you feel excited about a new project, then comes the roadblock of, ya know, actually starting. *What parts of me do I bring in? What is important or interesting? What will this really look like?* Rather than get deflated, take a deep breath, and let's work on this together.

These are
a few of my
favorite things.

QUESTION 1

What is your favorite ______?

I love to start with this question because it's a simple one everyone can answer. We can all name something we love, whether it's a color, a book, or a song. It's the perfect jumping-off point to get you scheming. To be clear, we are talking about physical things here, not necessarily activities or hobbies. (Do not fret. We will get to those!)

I typically like to start with color. Many people have trouble deciding on the hues they want in their home. They'll say, "Oh, I liked this teal bathroom I saw in a magazine," or "My friend has a yellow kitchen I like," followed by "But I worry I won't like it in a few years." All very normal, all very understandable. Color equals major commitment to many folks, and while studies have shown it demonstrates healthy psychology to change something significant in your home at least once every ten years, I get the hesitation.

Here's my little trick: Your best bet is to pick out colors you have always loved. Still confused? Pull out a box of crayons. You know the one—the big box with the sharpener. Find the colors you enjoyed as a kid. Most of the time they still hold true. Me? Cornflower blue all the way. I loved it then; I love it now. Clients may laugh when I pull out the Crayolas, but, hey, it's a great icebreaker.

Maybe you are someone who commonly uses a particular color range in your home and you are afraid to branch out. "I like orange," you may say, "but how do I use it?" Perhaps it manifests as a fruit in a fabric, or you cover an accent chair in a mandarin velvet. Work it in somehow!

Don't be afraid of what speaks to you in the color world—embrace it! Not everyone is meant to love an all-neutral room or whatever the trends are telling you to like. The world is a rainbow, and we are meant to live all along this spectrum. No fingerprint is the same, so let the fingerprint of your home show off its own unique shape. And if a certain color feels new and fun to you, and you want to test it out (even if it's just for a little while), try incorporating it in a small way: Paint a linen lampshade with fabric paint, glue trim onto the border of your curtains, go antiquing and find a pretty bowl or dish. Just go for it!

Enjoy the freedom you can find only at home. Maybe you have to wear a uniform to work—a belt that's too tight, uncomfortable shoes, or an unflattering color—but your home is a place to play, to experiment, to express yourself and exercise your creativity. What that looks like for you will be different from what it looks like for anyone else!

As far as favorites, color is a biggie, but it's not the only player on the field. Books, songs, even something as silly as a board game can spark a design plan. Think about favorite items in your wardrobe—maybe the things you love that you cannot seem to relinquish. Is there a striking pattern or graphic that grabs you? A friend of mine's favorite book when she was a child was Frances Hodgson Burnett's *The Secret Garden.* After she had her baby, she based her nursery around the colors dancing through her mind while rereading the story as an adult. The way she incorporated foliage motifs and botanical patterns made her room lovely, but the meaning made it *special.*

62 A client's love of emerald green is highlighted through the beadboard backsplash and island hue in her kitchen.
63 My husband and I both love birds. We enjoy looking at old ornithology books with their crisp, clean-line drawings. In our previous dining room, we chose a bird-filled wallpaper and used the matching fabric on the backs of the "mad hatter" chairs at each end of the table.

THE GLENLIVET
18
STRAIGHT RYE
LONGHAIR JIM
ACRE
ABERLOUR
10

Oh,
the places
you’ve been!

QUESTION 2

What places are filled with special memories for you?

This question is a fun one. People love to talk about their trips or memorable homes or places they have visited. Maybe what comes to mind is the lake cabin you went to as a child, or the place you stayed on your honeymoon, or your grandmother's kitchen—any sort of space that evokes an emotion within you. Tap into that. Bring it to the surface. Think of what you can do in your home to remind you of those feelings and memories.

Many clients have never contemplated how to incorporate a sentimental place into their home. But when I see clients answer this question with a soft gleam in their eyes as they share their recollections, I know they're telling me about a spot that needs to be recaptured in their home.

Don't be afraid to go fancy. Have you visited a place such as Marie Antoinette's grandiose home in Versailles or an esteemed architectural property that touched you? Reflect on that. Look back at your photos and pinpoint what felt exciting to you. Inspiration can come from any type of house—old or new, shack or chalet. Trim details, color combinations, old wallpaper patterns, antique tiles, the way a wood floor is laid—you can re-create anything you see that strikes you.

Edith Wharton was a famed American designer and author who penned classics such as *The Age of Innocence* and *The House of Mirth*. (By the way, if you're into period dramas, I highly recommend these novels.) She was one of the first designers to call for a more relaxed look and feel in the home, something I can definitely get behind. Coming out of the Victorian era, she believed rooms should appear less formal and more comfortable. She designed furniture to make you feel as though you could sink into it rather than perch upon it stiffly. The Mount, Wharton's gorgeous estate in the Berkshire Hills outside Lenox, Massachusetts, was one of my favorite early-marriage trips. There is a grand hall in Wharton's home, framed on both sides with soft-ivory walls accented with sage-green box trim. My husband and I loved the color combination coupled with the light coming in from the massive floor-to-ceiling windows. Feeling inspired, we tried to re-create this look in the office/workspace area of our old house. The space was just a small corner bedroom with lots of light—not nearly as grand as Wharton's great hall—but the scheme reminded us of that home and that trip. The details and ambiance became a little piece of those happy memories. A pretty terrific souvenir, I say.

Smaller spots in your home such as the laundry room pictured above are wonderful spaces to showcase a beloved trip. Who doesn't want to dream about coastal Italy while treating stains on soccer pants?

66 This couple honeymooned in Mexico and loved the bright-colored foliage patterns often seen in tile there. This feel was captured through the wallpaper that rises from behind the headboard and continues onto the ceiling.

67 A passion for horses led a couple to get engaged at a famed horse farm. These vintage stall doors operate as window treatments to close off the view when desired.

GRACE KELLY HOLLYWOOD DREAM GIRL

Show me
your stash . . .

QUESTION 3

Where is your box of mementos?

You know what I'm talkin' about: the box thrown into the back of your closet with notes, photos, and various memorabilia. Let's pull out those storage containers and have a look through them! Take note of what brings a smile to your face and set those items aside. After you are done, sort through what you placed in the "happy" pile. What stories and memories come up for you? What makes you laugh? What causes a little tear of remembrance? Don't hide those special happenings away—in your heart or in your home. Dust them off, bring them to the light, and share them with the people you invite into your space.

Most of the time these boxes hold a lot of paper. Handwriting is something I love to highlight when someone has a personal connection to notes and letters. The script of someone you love or want to remember is such an intimate, personalized memento, and there's something about displaying their penmanship (or scribble) that emphasizes and brings their words to life, even if the person has passed on. Mementos have that power: They share things about you that you could hardly say on your own. Maybe you have yellowed newspaper clippings of your athletic or academic endeavors, or letters between your grandparents during a war, or a sweet little card stamped with your baby's footprints, or even a silly photo you feel slightly embarrassed about. Show 'em off! Put a little ledge on the wall with thrifted frames and pop these treasures in. When you hear folks exclaim, "Oh my goodness, I didn't know that about you!", remember that by sharing yourself, you are opening the door for them to share themselves too. You are hoisting their freedom flag a little higher, and, hey, maybe you'll surprise (shock?) them a little. That's fun too.

LEFT This pantry showcases a beloved mother's transcription of party rules plus some of her special silver pieces attached to the walls. There are a variety of ways to make a space like this pretty, but take these mementos away, and it would not be as *meaningful.*

ABOVE LEFT While exploring ideas for an exterior makeover of her home, a client ruefully remarked on how quickly her children had grown as she fondly looked at their little handprints on the sidewalk. Tracing over the etched prints with chalk in the client's favorite color, yellow, and framing them as art brought these memories inside.

ABOVE RIGHT A couple's collection of special memories throughout their life together—baby bracelets and a baptism gown, concert tickets, nature finds, significant notes and letters, and more—came out of cardboard boxes and are now displayed in acrylic boxes in their bedroom.

Tell me
your family
folklore . . .

QUESTION 4

Do you have any interesting family history?

I've got quite a bit of Nancy Drew in me. I love to research! Tell me about your family lore and I am right on it—hunkering down at the computer, pulling up antiquated pictures, searching newspaper articles, researching previous home addresses. I piece together these fragments of information to formulate an outline of what someone's life has been like.

Sharing intriguing and surprising tidbits about family members in your home's design is a great way to give people insight into who you are and where you came from. Not only is it fun for people who visit you, but it also forms a bond between the past and the present. And don't we all want that: to remember, and to be remembered? There's something beautiful about the braided bonds of legacy and how your own loose ends tie in with the life you create day by day, year by year. The lasting effect of molding a family culture, loving your "bosom friends" well (as Anne would say), and being thoughtful about the people around you continues long after you are gone. Legacy inspires legacy, and highlighting it encourages you to be someone who sees yourself not as the main character in the story but as a person woven into the patchwork quilt of your community, many parts, all unique, all valuable, all interesting.

When a client shared her husband's long family history in a tiny Texas town, I got to researching right away. The husband's family were bankers, and they had a large hand in getting the little town off the ground back in the day. Consequently, they were quite beloved. When I found out the original 1900 bank building was dilapidated but still standing, I left home early one Saturday morning eager to make the four-hour drive to check it out for myself. Lo and behold, as I peered through the dirt-stained windows and looked past the caved-in ceiling, I could see the original marble counters and trim staring back at me. After I secured permission to salvage the pieces, my clients were overjoyed to find them installed in their brand-new bathroom—their own little piece of history, come home. I don't mean to make it sound easy, because it wasn't. There was no air-conditioning in this old bank building, and the temperature was 121 degrees! Not to mention the marble took great care and a hefty amount of labor to move. But it's a terrific story and something I will always be proud of. Is there anything valuable that doesn't require significant effort? Just think of the generations of fingerprints this marble touched. Now the stone and the memory are saved—old life with new use!

AMERICANA

LEFT A significant tablecloth exchanged between this couple's families during World War II is now framed in their living room.
UPPER LEFT AND LOWER RIGHT The salvaged marble from their family's bank is installed in this client's bathroom.
UPPER RIGHT AND LOWER LEFT A family's pride in their ancestors' founding of the town of Abilene, Texas, is displayed through the pictorial telling of the story. I used custom woodwork to frame the pages from a copy of their antique book in the entryway.

Show
and tell . . .

QUESTION 5

What are your hobbies, talents, and interests?

We live in an amazing world filled with amazing people. Sometimes I marvel at the various interests and talents of the clients I work with, though quite often homeowners are a little nervous to tell me about their hobbies or pastimes. Maybe they don't want me to know about their piccolo obsession and accompanying collection. Or perhaps they don't think they are very good at their hobby, so they want to keep it concealed. But you should not be ashamed of what makes you *you*, that little piece that fits only in your special puzzle.

As a child, I loved to jump rope. I was actually super good at it. I had a VHS tape (I still have it!) that demonstrated all sorts of cool tricks, and I was *into* it. Jump rope was relatively cool in the fourth grade, and when Ms. Gomez announced at PE that we were going to have a contest in the next two weeks, I was over the moon. She told us we were going to see how many consecutive jumps someone in our class could do. Nothing fancy, nothing tricky—just simple skips. As someone who felt as if she was always on the outside looking in (see the recollection of my BFG era), I thought, *Oh my goodness, I am so good at this! I will win for sure, and people will think it's neato! People will think I'm neato!* So, every night for fourteen straight days, I practiced my little heart out, taking care not to hit my headgear while jumping. The night before the contest, I asked to be excused from helping my dad cook dinner, and I skipped hundreds of times until my parents made me come inside to eat.

The next day, kids were skipping twenty times, fifty times . . . *I have this in the bag*, I thought. But—and I still have no idea what happened—on my very first jump, I tripped. I'll *never* forget Ms. Gomez calling out for all the class to hear: "Grace, one." I was in a complete state of shock and embarrassment. My one moment! My time to shine! How I wished for a hole I could crawl into!

The old jump rope I have in a shadow-box frame is a reminder of this funny, albeit humbling, story. And guess what: I still really enjoy jumping rope.

78 Ever since I was a little girl, I have loved pressing and labeling leaves and flowers I find. I framed this collection of antique botanicals and hung them from the original 1919 picture rail trim behind the bed in our previous home.
79 A homeowner's love of old cars and industrial design are on display in this kitchen.

THE HOLY BIBLE
THE STONEMASON
G

SMEG

In a world
of options,
likes are easy;
dislikes are
more helpful.

QUESTION 6

What do you not like?

We live in a world where we can view millions of lovely things at a click. While it's nice to be able to see beauty anytime we like, it can also feel overwhelming. So many pretty things to take in, so many appetizing options, so many styles to choose from—it can be very confusing! Therefore, a list of "don't likes" can be helpful.

I find this idea to be particularly helpful for folks who have a difficult time defining preferences. Often this is someone who *really* loves design. They watch *alllll* the shows, they subscribe to every design magazine, they love to rearrange their home. They can see many styles in their space, they find many colors thrilling, they can go so many ways! If this is you, narrow down how you want your home to feel to those few characteristics we talked about earlier, then weigh them against the design and decor elements you dislike. And don't accept any ol' thing. If you don't love it, if you aren't dying to get started, if what you see coming together doesn't thrill you, keep working at it. I have a pretty hard-and-fast rule about not settling. This is challenging at times, even for me. It's worth it to keep narrowing your focus on what will be a home that delights you for a long time.

ABOVE This family wanted their previously dark, windowless kitchen to be full of light, with no upper cabinets. A huge window addition meant the plates and bowls went in drawers with a peg system.
RIGHT This kitchen was designed for a client who said she did not like a lot of clutter on her kitchen countertops. With this in mind, even the appliances were tucked away in clever storage.

FRUIT
RECIPES
THAT
Appetizer

Cowboy,
take me
away.

QUESTION 7

What does your dream home look like?

Does this feel like a silly question to you? Does it feel nonsensical? To that, Anne Shirley would retort, "But just think what a dull world it would be if everyone was sensible." Maybe you would say your dream home is too far out of reach. Maybe it has a room where every wall is wrapped in hand-painted wallpaper, or perhaps it sports a fancy zip code. Or maybe you've been told it's a waste of time to dream at all. Let's set that thinking aside for a minute and start distinguishing the pieces of your dream home that might seem more accessible—and then try to make those happen. You may not be able to afford hand-painted wallpaper, but perhaps you can find that look. (There are some great options out there nowadays.) Maybe you could ask for some fancy towels and a cozy bathrobe for Christmas to get your dream bathroom going. Putting a little dream-home aspect into your house gives you a boost. Step-by-step, one day at a time.

A dear person in my life, Lila, told me her late husband often said, "Inch by inch, life's a cinch; yard by yard, life is hard." That has stuck with me, and it's now a common saying in our home. It may take some creativity, depending on what your aspiration is, but each little inch you move toward your dream home is a small step in creating the confidence it takes to reach your goals.

Maybe you remain unconvinced, and dreaming still doesn't sound like something you could do. Perhaps with the harsh realities you are facing, it seems impossible. Maybe because your story is hard, you don't want to think about dreams and goals. Most days just getting by seems good enough. I understand. After my car accident, after my miscarriages, after dealing with some deep grief in my early forties I had long avoided facing—these are all times when I didn't dare to dream, when I could hardly think of it. About a year and a half after my automobile wreck at twenty-two, I remember hanging out with my oldest brother, Christian, and his family, and him declaring with gentle joy, "Grace! You got your laugh back!" It still brings tears to my eyes to think of that moment.

All this to say . . . I understand how you feel. Draw near to friends you know you can rely on, keep your circle small and trust that circle with your muck, seek solace in family members who truly know you, find a counselor, and walk in faith that how you feel now is not how you will feel forever. There is always hope, and dreaming again can take a little practice. You may be rusty. You may not have exercised that muscle since you were a child. But there's something about the ability to dream that brings hope; there's something about having a "scope of imagination" (a frequent Anne phrase) that aids in seeing the goodness of life. And the truth is—no matter what your story is, no matter where you come from or where you have been, you can break the shackles that bind you, and you can shatter the power of whatever shackles others are bound by that have hurt you. You have the significance and the authority to create beauty around you—to spread kindness, joy, authenticity, freedom, and love. You get to rewrite the story, and it's never too late to start a new chapter.

"It's delightful when your imaginations come true, isn't it?"

—L. M. Montgomery, *Anne of Green Gables*

LEFT This client dreamed of a huge kitchen island, but the space could not quite support it without making an awkward flow. We split the worktable into two—one island holds the kitchen sink and one is more for entertaining.
ABOVE LEFT This client's penchant for natural stone led to this custom niche to hold bath products.
ABOVE RIGHT I had always envisioned herringbone floors in my bathroom, but the cost ended up being too high. When we renovated the primary bathroom in our previous home, my husband and I came up with the idea of using remnant tile and framing squares of herringbone to bring the total cost down to what we could afford.

TIDBITS OF ADVICE

"Isn't it splendid to think of all the things there are to find out about? It just makes me feel glad to be alive—it's such an interesting world. It wouldn't be half so interesting if we knew all about everything, would it?"

—L. M. Montgomery, *Anne of Green Gables*

While I imagine you picked up this book because you are into design, and perhaps you find my process intriguing, I wanted to be careful not to include information you could learn from an internet search—things such as the minimum amount of feet you should have around each end of your dining table (three) or how high the pendants above your island should be mounted (at least thirty-six inches). To do so would feel like a waste of the time we get together. I value every moment with you, and the fact that you are taking the time to read these words is meaningful to me. My goal is to provide a perspective you will not get anywhere else. So I put together a few personal notes on practicality in design. Don't worry, I've already made the mistakes for you—right inside my own home, a.k.a. the design lab. I hope these tidbits are helpful for you and lessen the worry and mystery of putting together a lasting space.

1. REGARDING WHAT EVERY ROOM NEEDS . . .

MY RECIPE FOR A WELL-LIVED ROOM:

ELEMENT(S) OF YOUR STORY

SOMETHING VINTAGE OR ANTIQUE

SOMETHING SLEEK

SOMETHING WOODEN

SOMETHING THAT EVOKES NATURE

SOMETHING "OFF"—A LITTLE QUIRKY OR UNEXPECTED

Note from me: The best rooms are the ones that look gathered and acquired over time—layer by layer. This list is not meant to be all-inclusive, by the way, but it's a great jumping-off point, and in my experience it covers the bases. It's also pretty flexible. No rigid rules here!

To give you an example of what this looks like, here's a peek into the imaginary living room I'm creating in my head right now. I would start by enlarging a beloved candid family photo and make that the art moment in the room. Perhaps it's in black and white with a simple frame. Underneath the picture, I'd place a well-made vintage sofa you bought at your neighbor's garage sale and have it covered in a modern fabric for the perfect juxtaposition of old and new. In front of the sofa, I'd put a metal coffee table laden with books, along with a large vessel containing a foraged branch or two. A pair of straight-lined chairs upholstered in a stripe would sit parallel to the sofa. On one wall would be an antique wooden chest of drawers in a lovely worn-oak finish, and on the other wall would be a marble pedestal found at the thrift store displaying your kids' favorite clay pieces from art class. Can you see it?

CONTRERAS DREAM DESIGN LIVE
MARKHAM ROBERTS

2. REGARDING PETS THAT SHED . . .

TAKE A LITTLE CLEAR BAGGIE OF THEIR FUR WITH YOU WHEN YOU GO SOFA OR RUG SHOPPING.

PLACE THE BAG AGAINST THE FABRIC OR TEXTILE OR RUG TO SEE HOW MUCH IT SHOWS.

Note from me: If you have animals and you don't want to live in a state of frustration over the fact that they do indeed have hair and shed, keep your baggie close by while you are shopping. In my experience with lots of families, I've noticed there usually seems to be one partner who is more into the pets than the other person, which can lead to some annoyance with animal evidence around the home. We have dogs that don't shed, but I use this advice in my own life too. (The olive velvet sofa pictured right seemed to repel dog hair, which was awesome.) Even animals that don't release hair daily can still leave their mark. Stain-friendly fabric is a great choice, but white hair on a dark color may get on your nerves. Decide what you can live with, do the hair check, and life will be better for all two- and-four-legged creatures in your house.

ZELDA

3. REGARDING PATTERN MIXING . . .

THE FOOLPROOF METHOD:

CHOOSE THREE COLORS, THEN PICK THE FOLLOWING PATTERNS THAT INCORPORATE YOUR HUES:

ONE SOLID

ONE STRIPE

ONE SMALL PATTERN

ONE LARGE PATTERN

(YOU DON'T KNOW HOW BADLY I WANTED A WORD THAT RHYMED WITH *STRIPE*. OH WELL.)

Note from me: This is the age-old "How do I mix color and pattern?" question. The above list is my go-to for a pleasant mix, but to get it right you'll need samples. Even I have a hard time putting patterns next to one another in my mind. (It can get pretty busy in there, anyway; I don't need chintz and plaid stirring the pot.) So take your time. Lay it all out. Let the samples sit, and look at them throughout the day (sometimes for several days!). Make sure to include at least one flowy motif in the small pattern or large pattern choice. And don't be afraid to toss in an item outside your color story, such as a throw blanket. Adding this "off item" helps a room feel more comfortable, less untouchable. When a room goes together too flawlessly, when a room matches perfectly, it can feel a little flat, which is not what we want. Homey yet chic, orderly yet not too perfect, warm yet not cliché—that's our aim.

4. REGARDING THE FIFTH WALL (THE CEILING) . . .

DON'T FORGET ABOUT IT.

Note from me: To give your room maximum sophistication, take your wall paint color and make it 50 percent lighter for your ceiling. The wall color will look darker on the ceiling, because the ceiling and walls are on different planes. Using this trick helps the colors flow seamlessly.

When it comes to interior design, I find the ceiling to be the most forgotten area. It's the top, the head over the body of your space. Sometimes I'll see a beautiful room with a lovely hue on the walls, amazing accents, and gorgeously curated art, and then—wham—my eyes stop at a white ceiling. Now, I'm not against a white ceiling—it works great if you have a white or light-colored room. But if you have color on your walls, a white ceiling can feel harsh. Coordinating the wall and ceiling colors creates a softer look and helps your room feel finished. And don't forget about the opportunity to use wallpaper—it's one of my favorite ways to add interest to a ceiling!

5. REGARDING COLORS YOU REALLY LOVE . . .

SEE QUESTION 1 (PAGE 61), BUT ALSO LOOK IN YOUR CLOSET.

Note from me: It's not all that unusual for people to be unsure of what colors they really want, especially if they feel a little windblown by whatever is the shade of the moment. I've had clients tell me they haven't painted their house in more than a decade because they were worried they would not like the color forever. Let me just release you from this concern: You will probably never like *anything* forever, and, in fact, you shouldn't. It is good and healthy to desire a change; it is a sign of positive mental health. (And please note I am referring to things and not humans.)

It's the same with fashion. Imagine if you wore all the same clothing your whole life, or if you never changed your makeup. We are not meant to be stagnant. It is a natural and normal thing to evolve and change, and to be excited by that. New dawn, new day!

If you feel completely befuddled when trying to figure out what you really want, take a look in your closet. It may sound strange, but when I have people bring me their favorite blouse or dress or piece of costume jewelry or tie or T-shirt, I not only get sentimental narratives but also discover color stories. The color story in your closet is more powerful than you think and can point the way to shades you naturally gravitate toward. Lay out your favorite items, photograph them together, and take it in—you may be surprised to see these colors go together beautifully!

6. REGARDING WHAT (AND WHAT NOT) TO SPEND MONEY ON . . .

YOU CAN MAKE A LIGHT OUT OF ALMOST ANYTHING.

YOU CAN FIND NEARLY ANY STYLE OF WALLPAPER AT ANY PRICE.

IT'S NOT DIFFICULT TO PAINT.

DECOR CAN BE MOSTLY ONE-OFF FOUND ITEMS.

DISHES AND KITCHEN ITEMS ABOUND AT THRIFT STORES.

POORLY MADE UPHOLSTERY IS A DAILY DISAPPOINTMENT.

Note from me: The cost of putting a home together can be daunting, I know. It feels defeating when you get excited about decorating your space, but then you go shopping and everything feels expensive and out of reach. Here are some questions to ask yourself when making home purchases:

- What does this say about me?
- Does it fit the person I am or desire to be? *(I am someone who ____.)*
- Does this suit the feeling I want to create in my home?

Completely decorating your home is definitely a long game. It can be hard to be patient, and it can also feel as though you will never get done, but, step-by-step, you will move closer to where you want to be. To avoid feeling overwhelmed, make a list of everything you desire to do room by room, and divide each room into doable sections. Keep this piece of paper so you can check off to-dos as they happen. It's so satisfying!

When I am designating funds on a tight project, I leave space for two things: one-of-a-kind finds that will set the project apart, and upholstery (for example, your everyday sofa). Nice upholstery that sits and wears well is worth paying more for. The piece may even come with a lifetime frame warranty, depending on the manufacturer. Good upholstery is an investment, and if you skimp on it, you're gonna feel it sooner than you hoped. If you don't wish to save up and buy new, keep an eye out at secondhand stores and local sale sites. Occasionally, I can even find a vintage sofa frame made by a well-respected vendor and have it re-covered for less than buying new. Of course, this depends on your fabric and upholstery cost, but it is doable.

7. REGARDING THAT FIND THAT JUST DOESN'T FIT (NOT RIGHT NOW, AT LEAST) . . .

IF IT'S TRULY SPECIAL AND UNIQUE, BUY IT.

YOU WILL ALWAYS FIND A PLACE FOR SOMETHING YOU LOVE.

YOU WILL NEVER REGRET BUYING (*CONSIDERED* BUYING, RATHER THAN IMPULSE BUYING), BUT YOU WILL REGRET NOT

Note from me: I have learned that when you turn a corner and see something that takes your breath away, you should buy it if you can afford it (even if you have to bargain a little). This typically happens to me at antiques fairs or flea markets, and believe me, when I haven't followed my own advice, I've regretted it. I have a mental list of things I regret not buying that haunt me a little to this day.

While I am not telling you to hoard things (I mean, maybe I am a little?), I do think that when you really love something, you will use it in your home. Also please note I am mostly talking about one-of-a-kind items, not mass-produced stuff. There are times when I purchase something thinking I may not have a spot for it right now, but it is too special or too great a price to pass up. Then, after I try the piece in a few different places, it finds a home. And, really, the things you love typically go together. It's funny how that works.

Procuring unique items—things no one else will have—is a part of making your home memorable. Those objects are instant conversation starters. So if you love it, and you can't stop thinking about it, chances are you should get it right then. If it is something amazing, someone else will think it's amazing, too, and then it's gone. And for you frequent antique shoppers, if you have never seen it, you probably will not see it again.

I don't want to leave you without hope, though. Even if the item sells before you can get back there, or you spot something already purchased, and you are heartbroken, here's a pro tip for ya: Don't give up easily! Leave the dealer a note with your phone number and a little message. The buyer may decide they don't want it after all, or you could even be corresponding with a dealer who wants to make some money. Throw in a little extra moolah if the buyer calls you, and walk away a winner. I've gotten a few items back that way, like the gorgeous brass kitchen cabinet in the house Leanne Ford and I designed together in Round Top, Texas. It makes for a great story, too, so win-win! Happy shopping—and may you keep that list of regrets as short as possible.

8. REGARDING MIXING YOUR STORY WITH YOUR PARTNER'S . . .

YOU LIKE TRADITIONAL; HE LIKES MODERN. THE MIX IS THE SECRET SAUCE—EMBRACE IT.

Note from me: One of the most frequent questions I get is about clashing styles between partners. I enjoy this type of challenge because I believe what people think is "bad" about having opposite design philosophies is actually a good thing. For example, I really like home fixtures with age—doors, windows, fireplace mantels, floors. But if I start with those elements as the background and add all old furniture or art, the room will feel flat. The patina on the older items will not stand out or feel special. On the other hand, when I mix in straight-lined furniture and some modern art, the space has depth and character; it feels layered and interesting.

The mix is truly to your benefit. No room that is all the same style and feel and texture reads well; we want to avoid one-note spaces.

Typically, I have both partners make a list of what's important to them, their vision and desires for each room, and then I compare the bullet points. Similarities make for easy compromise, but clear diversions bring big wins since mixing and matching opinions is the spice of life. Lean into those differences—that's when we create something unique and exciting!

9. REGARDING RENTING . . .

YOU CAN STILL PUT YOUR STORY IN A TEMPORARY HOME.

Note from me: Some advice we got from my husband's uncle still applies: Don't wait to make your home yours; that's a waste of time. Although I understand not taking the time or energy to put your story in a rented home, I do not think that's the way to go, and here's why: There's comfort and stability in feeling settled, a psychological boost. And your story stays with you no matter where you are.

Some people view renting as a step toward home ownership, and others, a worry-free lifestyle—either works. But I find some renters especially struggle with stagnancy because they are not where they want to be, thinking, *I'll cook when I have a nice kitchen*, or *I can't hang my photos—I won't be here forever*. This mentality is a symbol of something larger at play, a pervasive idea that's so common you may not even realize you are saying it to yourself: That where you are right now is not good enough. The "if only" of just about anything can tarnish the beauty you have in front of you right now. So what if you're not in your dream home? So what if you will move someday? So what if your kitchen is dated? You have the power to create the feel you desire in your home right now. You have the power to create a place you belong.

A storied home does not have to mean your forever home. Establish who you want to be in the home you live in, whatever that may be, in whatever circumstance.

1-16 oz can pumpkin
2 1/2 tsp pumpkin pie
1/4 c milk
PreHeat 350°
low speed 30 sec
Scrape bowl constantly
3 minutes
bake 50 minutes

10. REGARDING RESALE (IF YOU KNOW IT'S COMING SOON) . . .

MAKE YOUR STORY ELEMENTS LESS PERMANENT, BUT STILL HAVE THEM.

(DON'T BE SCARED OF PAINTING YOUR CABINETS OR WALLS.)

Note from me: Give me a moment while I step onto my soapbox and clear my throat. Ahem.

Buying a home is as hard as it's ever been, so once you do, you're less likely to move. Even so, nothing is forever. We get married, we change jobs, or we simply seek a change of scenery. Whatever the reason, it can seem like a waste to put much personality into a home just to leave it behind.

I get it.

But please understand you do not need to keep your whole house white or gray or beige to be able to sell it. In fact, homes with a little color and personality tend to sell better on average. If you want some color but are concerned about resale value, stick to colors reminiscent of the outdoors, like blues and greens, which seem to be more acceptable hues. And remember, your hard-earned money is going into the mortgage every month; this home is for you and your family. You're not just keeping it warm for someone else. So paint the walls if you want, change the hardware, add that cool pantry door, and, where you can, mix in some removable elements: Art, decor, furniture—anything that tells your story.

11. REGARDING KITCHENS AND BATHROOMS . . .

THESE ROOMS GET REAL COLD REAL FAST.

APPROACH THEM THE SAME WAY YOU WOULD A BEDROOM.

MAKE THEM FEEL COZY, COMFORTABLE, AND WARM.

Note from me: Kitchens and bathrooms are spaces for living, and making them appear homey and not sterile is continually a goal of mine. I want them to have a snuggly air, to be extensions of the comfortable rooms they're adjacent to. For example, the kitchen should feel like a continuation of the living room (assuming they're connected); the bathroom should feel like a continuation of the bedroom. That can mean putting a wood floor in the kitchen or, yes, even the bathroom! I realize that may scare some folks, but it is pleasant underfoot (never cold), and if you can get old-growth wood, the floor will last as long as you do. In bathrooms, I like to create vanities that resemble pieces of well-made furniture. Since tile, stone, and metal can give off an air of frigidity, I layer in softness wherever I can. Through the warmth of wood, the texture of drapery and rugs, the natural feel of wicker or sisal, or even the addition of a cozy chair or small sofa—any and all of these elements make a world of difference in the room-where-I-want-to-be factor.

Old European kitchens inspire me in the way they use furniture and fabrics you might see in other parts of the home. I love how they often feature raised-pattern tile and extra-thick marble counters that wear beautifully. If you get a chance to visit grand old homes in these countries, you will find marble counters hundreds of years old, with perfect patina telling the story of their use.

And while we are on the topic, please do not be afraid of marble and natural stone countertops and tile. Be sure to have your marble honed, then sealed, not polished—it wears better. (The glass-like finish on polished marble and stone tends to show spots and imperfections.) If you buy your stone slabs polished, you can have your fabricator hone them for a small fee.

Try approaching your kitchen and bathroom design the same as you would your living room or bedroom. I promise the results will be rewarding!

12. REGARDING ART . . .

IT CAN BE ANYTHING!

REALLY!

Note from me: While I love to support artists, there is not always room in the budget for high-priced art. I enjoy shopping local art shows because they feel like a treasure hunt. I also firmly believe you can make almost anything meaningful an art piece. After all, what constitutes art is subjective.

Take a sentimental sticky note, center it on an enormous mat, and place it in a large thrifted antique frame. Now you have something interesting and fun. At the home you see pictured to the right, I used a pretty pad of paper so the family and visitors could write what they were thankful for as a record of gratitude in their community.

At our previous home, I turned a favorite photo of our kids at the beach into a mural and wrapped it around the wall above the mantel. I peeled it off, rolled it up, and took it with us when we moved.

What about displaying a special collection in a sleek modern frame? Or maybe form a shape out of old polaroids taped to the wall? Get creative and shoot for something uniquely you. Most of all, have fun!

I am thankful for
Family
I am thankful for
God's provision

SO . . .
WHAT'S
IT LIKE?

family stories

"It takes all kinds of people to make a world."

—L. M. Montgomery, *Anne's House of Dreams*

For over fifteen years, I have been an advocate for designing homes around personal stories—autobiographical design, if you will. Of course, I know what this has looked like for my family, but what about for my clients, the families who have had the experience of implementing their stories into their homes? How has it affected them? Has it changed how they feel? Was it worth it in the end? Here are some of those stories, written through the lens of the people who have been through the transformation. Beyond a rearranged room and a missing wall or two, beyond a set of bay windows, new paint, salvaged doors, and lights made from things you wouldn't expect, the story goes on. The anticipation of how everything will come together is past, the newness of the project has worn off, and with a lot of time now spent living in their storied homes, these clients are relaying their perspectives.

To those who agreed to share their stories with me (and now with you), thank you—I am honored to be a small part of them. I want you to know that your stories—filled with so much courage and hope and wisdom and fun—have enriched mine, and I am grateful to all of you.

THE NOKESES' STORY

Although I love working on hundred-year-old homes, I also relish working on more modern spaces. When I laid eyes on the Nokeses' 1960s lake house, I was immediately excited. Word on the street (or, rather, the lake) was this house had been quite the party palace back in the '60s and '70s, even hosting famous musical groups such as the Bee Gees! The home felt wet and aged, but underneath the bad tile and dated fixtures was a gem waiting to shine again.

Ruth and Bryson, the homeowners, loved the water, and Bryson especially enjoyed fishing. They both wanted to capitalize on the groovy vibe of the era in which their house was built but add a modern, industrial flair.

When Ruth, a successful family photographer, lamented the fact she had no recent photos of her own family, my mind started churning. I had long been a fan of the famous photographer Slim Aarons and his stylized shoots depicting mid-century life, especially glorifying pools and parties. That type of illustration felt like the perfect backdrop to this home and its history. In the living space, where we would install a huge wall of glass doors to take in the amazing view of the water, there was also a rather funky fireplace wall. It seemed to be the perfect place to make a statement, such as an oversized family photo, Slim Aarons–style.

I envisioned the shoot, settled the details to make it happen, and searched for the main prop I needed: a beautiful vintage wood canoe, which I eventually found on a local resale website. Bryson and their son were instructed to wear their favorite fishing clothes, within certain color parameters so everything would coordinate but not be too perfectly matched. Meanwhile, I headed to a local costume shop to pick up a few "flower power" dresses that fit the vibe so Ruth could pick her favorite to wear. The Nokes family was a little nervous about how this would turn out, but they were into the idea. Although the day we shot was actually freezing, the photos turned out spectacular and created a unique statement perfectly suited to this family.

For the perfect *wow* moment, after the photo shoot we transformed the canoe into a light fixture and hung it over the living space. Hoisting it up the very tall ceiling and installing it securely was quite a harried event, but goodness, it was worth it. (My kids still talk about picking up this canoe and driving with it mounted to the top of our car for school drop-off.) It is a story-filled experience to walk into the Nokeses' home now!

MARY MCDONALD INTERIORS
ONE HUNDRED BUTTERFLIES

Living in a home that told our family's story changed everything for me. It wasn't just a house anymore; it became a living connection to our past, a constant reminder of how we came to be. Every detail, every room carried a piece of who we were, and that gave the place a weight far beyond nostalgia. It was our anchor, the foundation of our memories.

Through this process I realized just how crucial it is to have a true home. Not just a house to sleep in, but a space that feels like the heart of your life. I had always loved style, often prioritizing aesthetics over comfort, but this experience taught me that I didn't have to choose between the two. I learned how to create a home that we could truly live in, not just admire.

Beyond size or style, my home has shaped the way we live our lives. I feel that loving my home allows others to love being here too. It has become the setting for our most cherished moments, a place where memories are made in real time. Our best conversations unfold here, around meals with loved ones, as we gather to laugh and talk. Creating a storied home, I've learned, isn't just about preserving the past—it's about cultivating a space where the present feels just as meaningful. It's a feeling of comfort, peace, and belonging. Our house is more than a home—it's the heart of our life.

—Ruth Nokes

FRESH & EASY
Small Victories

THE FINDLEYS' STORY

When I met the Findley family, they had been through something every parent fears—the extended illness of a child. Their young son suffered a stroke, and everything changed. Though they had some scary moments and were a little unsure of the future, they made it through those excruciatingly difficult months. As their son healed and grew stronger, they felt more ready to begin the major home renovation they had been forced to wait on.

Listening to them and their story, I was inspired by their willingness to share what they had walked through. Most of all, I was inspired by their hope. Reading Lauren and Robert's words in their questionnaire instantly gave me a vision of their home—happy, hopeful, and full of light. "We have learned through our time with Ethan's stroke that even in the darkest of times there is still light that outshines the darkness," they wrote. "We really want our house to reflect hope, joy, love, and light. We want a place that makes people want to drop by. We want them to feel comfortable, inspired, hopeful, and joyful."

Because Lauren and Robert married at the beach and loved to vacation there, I knew their kitchen should evoke a relaxed feel, reminiscent of water and sand. A rough-textured white tile, navy-blue cabinets, and a vintage-inspired cast-iron sink outline the space. Antique copper and brass ship lights, their cords wrapped in rope, hang over the island, at the end of which is a slipcovered bench for their two boys. The bench lends some softness to the space, not to mention practicality with its washable cover.

Lauren shared her wish for easy-to-reach plates and glasses but wasn't sure about going with open shelving. While wandering my local salvage yard, I found an old convenience-store set of metal refrigerator shelves and turned them into a countertop cabinet. Everything is displayed, simple to access, and the overall look suits the beachy vibe.

Both Lauren and Robert deeply desire their home to be a comfortable haven for others—they want it to be a place where anyone can grab a plate, sit at the table, and share their life. The vintage plates mounted on the wall echo this sentiment.

In their living room, the old fireplace was refurbished to be double-sided with the dining space, and the ceiling was clad in a wallpaper featuring swallows, the symbol of hope. When I found some of Robert's impressive drawings, I set up a little art area by the window for him. He could be near his family and also practice his talent.

Finally, the word *hope* was placed above their fireplace mantel. It fits them so well, as a family who has gone through an intensely difficult trial, who believe so much in hope and can now share it with every person who comes through their door. What an inspiration to all!

hope

We had always planned to renovate our 1940s home but didn't know where to start. Once our son had a stroke in 2017, those plans were placed far on the back burner. Our home had good bones, but it was dark and dingy, and the layout was not well planned. Before the renovation, our kitchen space was pretty much a fire hazard, and the rest of our home felt dark and dirty no matter how much cleaning and sprucing we did. After renovating our home, we finally felt good enough to host family and friends. But it was more than just excitement over having our house renovated—we got to share us.

Because of what you see just upon coming through our front door (the word hope is hung over the fireplace, which is the first thing most people notice), our house became a place of joy and thankfulness, as it constantly reminds us of the light that shone through the darkness during the most difficult of times. We actually felt like the space became a constant act of worship for the God who has always been so good to us. When someone enters our home, we are able to share our journey through dark times, the meaning behind our home, and the light it now shares. It's easy to gloss over difficult experiences or want to bury them to an extent. We didn't realize how important it would be to us to live in a place that was more than just beautiful. Our home now shares our personal story through the walls.

—Lauren Findley

Galerie
Le compte
des photos qui y
beaucoup moins.
Certaines
et d'aujourd'hui
d'autres,
Picasso, Leonardo DiCaprio,
d'hier
Marilyn Monroe, Barack Obama, Sophia Loren ou encore Bob Dylan.
ÉTUDE POUR TISSU À MOTIFS DE PARASOLS,
Attitude
IS EVERYTHING
Je vais bien, tout va bien
2017 marque le 160e anniversaire de la naissance du pharmacien Émile Coué, inventeur de la méthode d'autosuggestion avec la fameuse formule à répéter vingt fois matin et soir : "Tous les jours, à tout point de vue, je vais de mieux en mieux." L'occasion de (re)découvrir cette technique pionnière qui a ouvert la voie aux différents courants de développement personnel contemporains.
56
52

THE SCHULZES' STORY

Erin and Charlie Schulz and their two kids are the kind of people you feel drawn to immediately when you meet them. Hearing their story of being college sweethearts and seeing the obvious love they share endeared them to me instantly. Their ranch-style home was ripe and ready to move on from its *Brady Bunch*–era kitchen, and the good news was they had plenty of space to spread out. Their floor plan needed major rearranging, which invigorated me, because creating an efficient and practical layout is one of my favorite games to play.

The Schulzes' alma mater, TCU, held a lot of special memories for them, and I was delighted to hear of Charlie's hidden talent—photography. He had taken images of Erin's and his sentimental landmarks around the campus and wanted to use them in their home but wasn't exactly sure how. I ended up turning the photos into wallpaper lining the fronts of the cabinets in their home office.

Erin and Charlie desired a sleek, industrial kitchen, and I softened it up by reusing the bricks salvaged from their old kitchen walls. Charlie is a member of the family behind Isaly's, the long-standing dairy product (the family invented the Klondike bar!) and restaurant chain, and I knew we needed to pay homage to that. A small room off the kitchen was the perfect place to add a swerve-seat table and vintage malt shop set, along with something else that brought back beloved memories. Erin shared the love letters she and Charlie had written in college, giving me permission to display them in their home. Their words are a dear reminder of young love but also of lasting kinship. Turning them into wallpaper that bordered this special little room made the space feel so intimate, almost sacred.

To further extend this idea into the next generation of their family, I placed maple clipboards monogrammed with each of their names near the breakfast nook, encouraging them to continue writing notes to each other. What a beautiful example to their kids and everyone else who comes into contact with them, and an everyday reminder of what has been and what will continue!

so bright I cannot wait to see what it brings our way. You make everything I do worth while. All my love. You are my best friend & I love you with all my heart.
ups and downs but the good times have far outweighed the bad. Our future is so bright I cannot wait to see what it brings our way.
much we both love each other
fect woman I would rather spend my life with
d & I love you with all my heart I love you.
you mean the entire world to me. You are my best friend.
is true and it will only
for the time
it to see
nt thing of a
both love

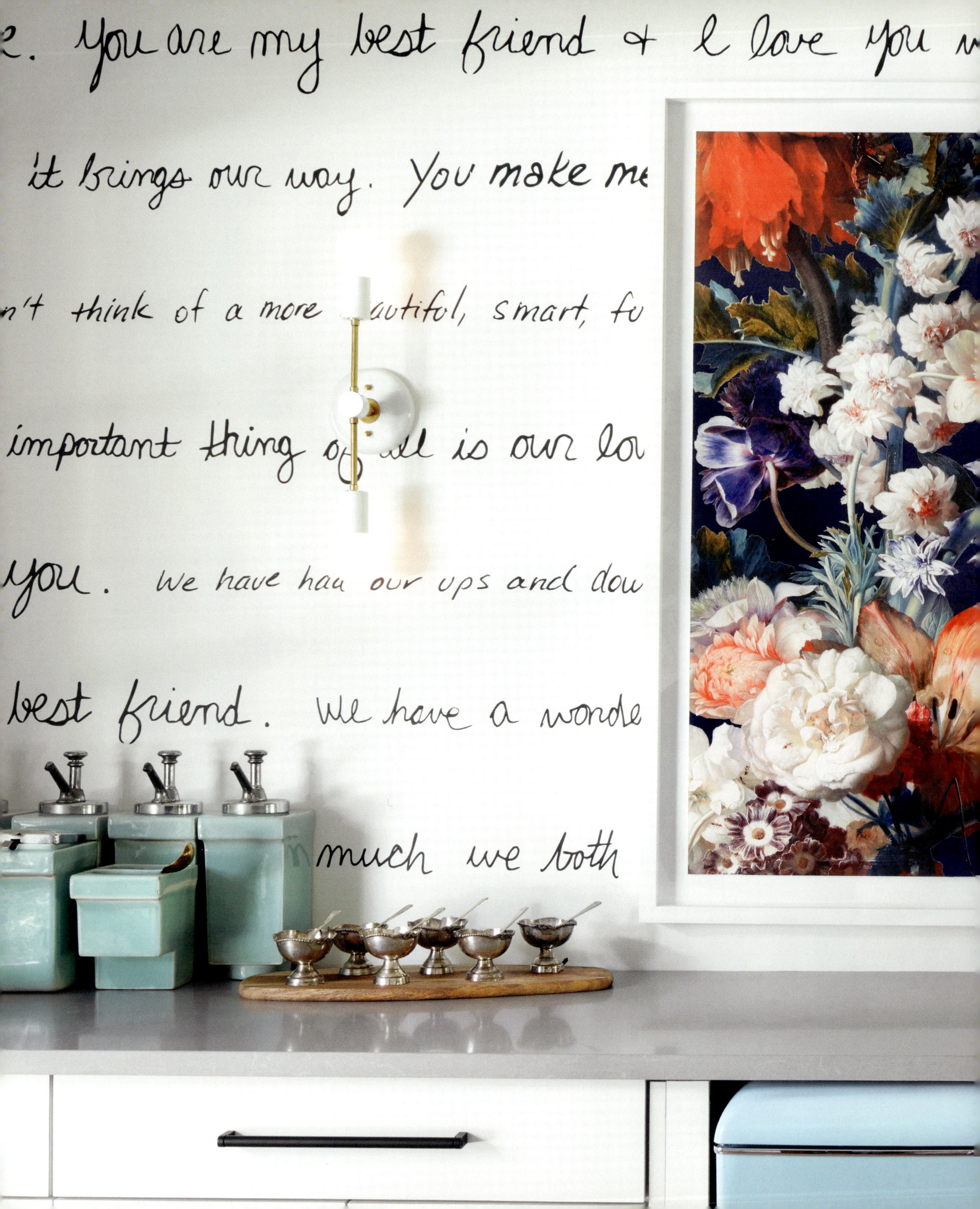

You are my best friend & I love you
it brings our way. You make
think of a more smart,
important thing is our
you. We have had our ups and
best friend. We have a
much we both

th all my heart. I am so thankful for the time we ha
d. you mean the entire world to me.
er spend my lif with. I Love you. Our fu
et stronger. you make me happy when
veighed the bad. ... just remember ha
love. You make everything I do worth
I am so th have

BREAD

love notes
ERIN
CHARLIE
COLBIE
MADDON

I Shall Always Love You Schweetie

I Shall Always Love You Schwe

RISCKY'S BAR-B-Q
NATIONAL CHAMPIONS 1935 1938
SUGAR BOWL
WELCOME TO AMON G. CARTER STADIUM
INDEPENDENCE BOWL
MOBILE ALABAMA BOWL

Where do I even begin? Thinking through the story of us provided a home that exemplifies all the details we enjoy most about our family: spending time together, playing games, cooking and eating meals together, entertaining. Each personal detail in every single room is a reminder of where we came from and the life we have built together, from the picture overlays on the cabinets in Charlie's office to our college love letters wallpaper in the eating nook in the kitchen.

We now *love* sharing our home with others! One area of the kitchen space is designed as an ice cream parlor—a personal tribute to Charlie's side of the family owning a dairy and ice cream shop called Isaly's. At Christmas, this space serves as the perfect spot to set up a cocoa bar and decorate Christmas cookies. It is so fun, and we love how it sparks interesting conversations among the kids and their friends about our family history!

Because Charlie and I are both open books, I was not really worried about designing our home around our story, although it is definitely an interesting process to figure out how to use various aspects of "our story" throughout the home. Not only do we get to share our space but we also get to share *us*. It's a good feeling. Each part of our house truly reflects what is meaningful to our family—now and for years to come.

—Erin Schulz

SKETCH BOOK
Welcome Home

THE HUNTS' STORY

When I arrived on the scene at the Hunt house, Lee and Sarah had really been through it. A flood had devastated part of their home, and while the event was distressing, I was impressed with their positivity. They felt frustrated, of course—this would be hard for anyone—but they were excited to move on and tackle some long-awaited projects. Namely, their primary bedroom and bathroom. Their sense of gratitude touched me as we dug in together to create the suite of their dreams. And when I found out we could enclose an unused back porch to expand their bathroom and closet, we were off to the races.

Lee and Sarah had lived in a space that suited them so poorly for so long that they stated, "Anything will be an improvement." They wanted a textured, layered bedroom with a little color. Lee was eager to surprise Sarah with a fireplace they could see from bed, but the space was a little tight because it was also a walkway to the bathroom. After a little outside-the-box thinking, we made the space functional and the fire surround beautiful by placing a gorgeous shaped tile around the perimeter instead of butting into the space with a typical mantel. My wonderful friend and beautiful artist Kelly Kay created the book art behind the bed (Sarah is a teacher and a book lover), with each book title signifying something special about Lee and Sarah's life together. In the bathroom, mirrors made from wine barrels represent some favorite trips, and Sarah got the deep tub that reminded her of her grandmother's, which she felt she could swim in as a child. Wanting to add an element of their story to the living space, I commissioned another beloved artist friend, Madison Phipps, who traced in the stain of coffee grounds the downtown outlines of every city where Lee and Sarah had lived together. The palette choice was in honor of their original meeting place—a coffee shop, of course.

SUNDAY SUPPERS
HABITAT

Our previous homes, to me anyway, were always sort of a means to an end. For our family, style took a back seat to utility. Being "right for us" had far more to do with our circumstances at the time of our move—budget, distance to the office, proximity to family, and so on. It was never reflective of who we were, what we liked, and where we've been—these elements simply were not a consideration.

One obvious reason may be that so much of our story had not yet been written. The places we'd go we had not yet been. The friends we'd make were still strangers. We were largely defined by what we did for work: a cop and a teacher. But as our story continued to be written, and we left that which we knew for that which we did not, additional facets of our life began to take shape. Our experiences came to define what it meant to be "us."

When our Fort Worth home flooded, we initially viewed that circumstance purely as a source of stress and grief. Shortly, though, that gave way to opportunity: We could make our house a home that reflected our family's personality while better meeting our needs. From city skylines painted in coffee to bathroom mirrors fabricated from wine barrels, each element of our storied home tells of our family's journey together. Our home transformed into another symbol of that journey: a happy consequence of an otherwise unfortunate circumstance.

Post-renovation, we've been presented with a number of opportunities for change: jobs in other cities, jobs in other states. We've elected to stay put, though. It takes a lot of thought, time, effort, and expense to turn a house into a home. We continue to love coming back home to our story. The experience, and the home itself, provide us with roots to the community and to our address we are unlikely to find elsewhere.

—Lee Hunt

THE HORCHNERS' STORY

When I met the Horchners through my good friend and real estate agent Jeremy Davis, I knew they were wonderful people. Their warmth, family-centric ethos, and authenticity shone from every word they spoke about their lives. Like many wise buyers, Todd and Maria purchased the worst house in the best location. And their location was really amazing—on the lake, with a dock (although dilapidated), a sport court (even more dilapidated), and plenty of hangout space. It was the perfect place to gather, and that was their exact vision. The property was simply in need of a lot of love and attention.

Achieving their dream of living in a lake house had been a long time coming and was hard-earned. With one daughter in college and one soon to graduate, they knew they wanted an abode where they could host lots of friends and family. Surely the allure of a comfortable lake home would entice kids to come home and bring plenty of their friends! "The lake is our happy place" was a phrase that appeared a few times throughout their questionnaire. But Todd and Maria did not want a cliché lake house—no oars or floats on the wall. Their desire was for the home to honor the outdoors they loved: Blue water and skies, green grass and plants, and water-worn wood.

Close to the lake, a small run-down outbuilding with a breezy outside porch caught my eye, and the family was excited about the idea of creating a hangout space there. And create it we did! By making a mini kitchen, incorporating a fridge and long counter for serving up snacks and smoothies, we made the space feel just like a cabana by the beach. A treasured photo of their young girls printed on tile (yes, actual tile!) was the perfect finishing touch, not to mention quite practical for a wet area.

Inside the home the kitchen posed a conundrum. As much as I wanted to open it up to get that gorgeous lake view, per the Horchners' request, I found out we would have to incorporate support columns. Not my favorite design element, as you can imagine. But we solved the problem by using weathered antique beams to frame out the island area. To play off the warmth of the wood, we painted the island a deep olive, adding glass-front drawers equipped with a peg system inside for easy plate and cup storage. A blue glass refrigerator portrays a watery feel, neutral cabinets balance the space, and a textured tile gives the kitchen that slightly bohemian touch. The dining area adjacent to the kitchen houses an extra-long antique dining table ready to host large dinners, illuminated by the organic nest-like orb mounted above. Having the custom "Team Together" (a phrase I heard the Horchners repeat) neon sign made by my always-up-for-it-and-will-figure-it-out friend Joe Mello added a fun factor to the room. It's a lake house after all—fun is in order!

Moving to the primary bedroom and bathroom, I kept the resting space light and ocean-airy by painting the walls a soft shade of water: a soothing greenish blue. Because of the Horchners' fond memories of Pine Cove family camp in East Texas among the tall, swaying pine trees, a dove-gray wallpaper with a light pine-cone print decorates the ceiling. For the bathroom, they requested a getaway feel. Tadelakt walls, a deep copper tub, a large window for taking in the private waterscape, and the overall ambiance allow for a peaceful exhale you can hardly resist when entering this room. An upstairs bunk room and cheery bathroom complete this dream home, ready for many years of wonderful memories.

Appetizer

Team Together

Living in a storied home has helped me feel confident to invite neighbors over for dinner and games, opening up to them while sharing life. I've discovered how much I enjoy entertaining! The home reflects who we are and what is important to us.

Living in a storied home has provided joy, confidence, and peace, and creates amazing, fun moments. The oasis for our daughters upstairs with custom bunk beds and a hangout area for friends has been an incredible addition to our family life. Windows line the upstairs bunk room as it overlooks the lake and nature reserve. Our daughters have spent many mornings enjoying the sunrise and relaxing. We are beyond thankful for the beautiful design of our lake home, a gathering place, showcasing the essence of who we are.

—Maria Horchner

Capitol
GRACE KELLY - FRANK
HIGH SOCIETY
Louis Armstrong and His Band
and Music by Cole Porter
SOCIETY (OVERTURE)
Orchestra
HIGH SOCIETY CALYPSO
Armstrong and His Band
3. LITTLE ONE
Bing Crosby
WANTS TO BE A MILLIONAIRE
Sinatra - Celeste Holm
5. TRUE LOVE
Crosby - Grace Kelly
Green Conducting the
G-M Studio Orchestra
PLAYING
HOLLYWOOD

THE ABRAHAMS' STORY

Katy and Joe Abraham are the type of people you just want to sit down and be with. They are personable, funny, interesting—and, goodness, do they love their dogs! Dog people are good people, and I was touched listening to them describe each one of their beloved pets. The Abrahams' 1950s home had been renovated piece by piece, and these homeowners were ready for the next phase—a new primary suite, a powder room revamp, and a fresh look for their living room.

The Abrahams have done extensive traveling and wanted their bedroom and bathroom to feel like a fancy hotel. Upon discovering we could raise the ceiling in both the bedroom and the bathroom, they were very excited! A soft-blue striped wallpaper washes down the walls of their bedroom, even across the doors to the bathroom accented with sparkling glass knobs. The tall peacock velvet headboard and burled-wood nightstands add a luxe feel to the space, along with the chaise for lounging. With the new height in the bathroom, I was able to incorporate an unbelievable barrel-vault ceiling, laden with glimmering tile all the way around the room. Being in the space almost feels like visiting the inside of a diamond, with gorgeous dapples of light reflected everywhere you turn. The custom cabinetry with a hidden vanity area and arched mirrors add to the elegant oasis. A luxury bedroom suite indeed, on par with a ritzy hotel, I'd say!

For the Abrahams' powder room makeover, I installed a rather dignified dog wallpaper, along with a glamorous brass-and-marble sink. The living room, however, is where we had the most fun. After seeing how much Katy and Joe cherished the photos of their previous pets, I decided to hire a dog photographer for a photo shoot with Sunny, their cream-colored Labradoodle. Now, I have styled many a shoot, but this one was a first for me! It took a lot of energy, but we came out with some terrific images for Joe and Katy to treasure for years to come.

One of the reasons I love my job so much is that no story is ever retold. Each family's unique set of characteristics always reveals a new outlook in each home.

WAYNE NEWTON
RED ROSES FOR A BLUE LADY

Our home is not only a place illustrated with our favorite colors but also a space reflective of what is in our hearts. Joe and I share our home with our true loves—our dogs. Spanky and Darla have passed on, but incorporating life-size photos of our newest baby, Sunny, in the living space brings us such joy. As you can imagine, striking a balance between Labradors and a chic living space is challenging; however, we adore that the most perfect reflection of our love for our babies and the most elegant and functional space can exist in harmony.

We love to travel, and choosing where to stay is always exciting for us. Putting elements of our favorite hotels into our home has been such a dream. It's not a stretch to say I'm impressed every time I walk into my bedroom and bathroom. Guests who have been over multiple times still ask to see the bathroom! Now we are very "house proud," eager to share our beautiful space with those we love. It has made a huge impact on our life.

Reflecting on our personal memories, milestones, and the journey we've experienced has been deeply insightful. A home that mirrors our story has become a haven that feels personal and comforting. For Joe, Sunny, and me, crafting a home that illustrates our story allows us to honor our past, acknowledge our growth, and embrace our identity. It might mean surrounding ourselves with objects that hold sentimental value, photographs that capture meaningful moments, or elements that represent different phases of life. Every corner of the space has become a living testament to our personal journey. The impact of such reflection can be profound. It often brings a sense of peace and belonging. Our home has become more than just a space we inhabit—it's a place that holds emotional significance and grounds us.

The lessons learned from having a home that reflects our story include a deeper connection to our values, a greater appreciation for the journey we've taken, and a clearer understanding of the things that matter to us. We've realized that our physical environment plays a huge role in shaping our mental and emotional well-being, and that consciously curating our space can positively influence our life. We are so thrilled with our home!

—Katy Abraham

THE MAYOS' STORY

I loved Mary Mayo and her family from the moment I met them. She could not wait to "talk shop" and show me all her interesting finds waiting in the garage for their moment in her home—a kindred spirit indeed! She loved hunting for vintage home decor, crafting, striking a good deal, and, most of all, spending time with her family. She was bubbly, fun, and a delight. And, boy, did she have a story.

I remember our initial meeting so vividly. She told me of the passing of her first husband and father to her three children, and of her raising Ty, Charlie, and Joy alone as a young widow—that is, until she became reacquainted with a college friend, Geno, and remarried. Shortly after, Mary was diagnosed with cancer, which she was fighting with all her might when we met. This family had put many projects on hold, but they were ready to tackle a new chapter of their home. Everyone was excited, and I was too. It's not often I come upon someone who has more projects waiting in the garage than I do!

A few weeks after our meeting, Mary texted me. She felt that with all she had going on with her treatments, it was the wrong time to start such a large renovation. I was sad to hear this, as I was so looking forward to creating with their family, but I understood. "Keep praying on it," I told her. "I would love to work on your home, but do what's best for your family."

Imagine my surprise days later when Mary messaged me, "We're in!" I called her immediately, and she shared what changed her mind—her youngest daughter, Joy. In all her sweet ten-year-old spunk, with her cute bobbed hair and round glasses, Joy had said to her family something like, "Let Grace do her thing and stop worrying and asking questions. It is time to do it, and nothing is going to change around here unless we get started."

"Well, thank goodness for Joy," I said with a laugh—and I meant it. I'll never forget Joy's excitement the day we started demolition—her hair and her whole petite self happily bouncing up and down in the window as she watched for me. She ran outside and gave me a giant hug. And I bounced with her.

Besides crafting, Mary also enjoyed flower arranging and had consequently amassed a large vase collection. Creating a space for her to retreat to and house all her supplies, while still providing some practical family storage, was a challenge I embraced. Plus, I got to enjoy it with Mary after the project was complete, as she taught me to make her favorite crafts—oh, what sweet memories!

I had long envisioned the idea of glass-front drawers for pretty storage (and perhaps as a motivator to stay organized), and this was the perfect place to try it out—an idea I've since implemented in my own house. All the craft supplies had a spot, and they were lovingly placed by my master-at-organizing friend, Jen Jones.

The Mayos loved nature and anything outdoors, and they especially wanted to add more wood elements to their home. A pair of enormous stumps found by the side of the road were a prized possession. Both Mary and Geno had spent hours hacking off the old bark and sanding them smooth. Mary worked with gusto since she was thrilled to save something old and make it into something beautiful, and Geno sanded and sanded because

he loved Mary. After the stumps were sealed and dry, they were the last items we placed in the living room. The weight alone made moving them nearly impossible, but Mary was right: They were perfect. We cut one of the leftover stumps into slices and created a gorgeous entryway ceiling.

Geno is a pilot, and Mary excitedly shared a photo of an old set of airline seats a college roommate gifted her. "Help me find a place in the house for these!" she gushed. (They both wanted elements of industrial design throughout the home.) Those seats became the counter stools for the Mayos' new kitchen island. And Mary's dream of a kitchen in which to entertain and connect with the people she loved came true. A room off the living space became a kids' hangout and study area, and with its custom-built Murphy bed made by my carpenter friend Jen Woodhouse, it can also be used as guest quarters. The first Thanksgiving after the renovation was complete, Mary texted me this message, and I'm so glad I saved it: "We are hosting Thanksgiving lunch, and I just had to come to the back of the house to text you to say thank you. You made me a real live hostess with a dream kitchen."

It was only a few short weeks later we got the heartbreaking news that dear Joy had been killed in an accident. There are no words for an unfathomable loss like this, and our community wrapped Mary and Geno and the kids in our arms and in love. It cut so deeply, and it still hurts. But words Mary shared will never leave my memory and heart: "We had no idea how much we would need a haven," she said. "A place to comfort us and for people to come to be comforted. A place I didn't have to worry about things working or a to-do list. We could just be—in our happy memories and in our grief. I look back, and it's like Joy knew what we would need. But I know that's not right—it was God who knew." A year and a half later, Mary passed from this life, and I just know Joy was waiting for her, her bobbed hair bouncing up and down.

To Geno, Ty, Charlie, and family—being a part of your story is one of the most blessed parts of mine. You are loved. And Mary and Joy—I will carry you with me in my heart forever. I'll see ya when I get there, and we will make the most beautiful crafts with all the glitter and yarn in every color, I have no doubt!

A very special thanks to Geno for sharing his story.

Crayola
Crayola

M
G

ALL GOOD THINGS
ORGANIC SEEDS
Buttercrunch Lettuce

if you want to
bring happiness
to the whole
world, go home and
love your family
MOTHER TERESA

Old
New
Bird poop.
Thank you!
what if...
boy
you
mr.rick
ms.beky
Grace
Please write back!!
Dear grace,
Thank you so much for all you have done. My family greatly appresh;ates you Grace.
God gave you your amazing talent and you really do deserve it. You have started an amazing new chapter in our lives.
XOXO, Joy
MM

Before the renovation, we viewed our home as a sort of base camp and spent as much time away from home as possible. Mary would often say, "I just don't want to be home today." When the work was finished, it became a refuge from the challenges we were facing. Mary finally had a place to relax and enjoy her crafts, and we had room to entertain guests when she felt well.

Mary was always very open about her battle with cancer and the many ups and downs we experienced. I tended to keep those trials more private. Now, two years after she passed, I've continued to share our story as she did. So many parts of our home, like the tree-stump coffee tables, beg us to share memories of Mary and Joy.

Many details in our home spark conversations about our life and story. Most are good memories, and some are really hard; but, either way, our home allows us to share parts of life with others we might often keep to ourselves. Not sharing those parts of our story would be a great tragedy. The good memories are even sweeter when shared, and acknowledging the difficult memories brings healing to us and encourages those who walk through them with us.

I've discovered I actually enjoy sharing our story with others. We have endured substantial suffering in the past five years, but God has been faithful and surrounded us with a community of believers who encourage us at every turn. Mary often discussed with me her goal to show the kids that, despite the trials in our life, God is good, and He can be trusted. Through His grace, I'm confident that Ty and Charlie believe that truth and have made it a goal of theirs to share that with others.

This project was more than opening up spaces in our house; we ended up opening our lives to those around us. Over the past five years, we have lived in rich community with our neighbors and formed deep connections with friends and family in our storied home.

—Geno Mayo

BRING THE OUTDOORS IN

We are not meant to live a life filled only with surface conversation, where people don't really know more than the most superficial things about us, and we are not meant to have homes that are just pretty little boxes, fit for anyone and everyone but no one in particular.

Stories are connectors. They connect us to one another, they connect us to the past, and they are bridges to the future. And, in many ways, our stories are gifts—of joy and sorrow, hope and healing, risk and gain and loss—all meant to be shared. I love reading about the prehistoric drawings that archaeologists find on cave walls. These etchings were really the first home decor—the stories of their lives painted in pigment on ancient limestone walls. Incredible! Who knew a hole in a mountain could be so chic?! There's something so human about sharing ourselves with others—opening the door to who we are, where we've been, where we may be going—that can have a lasting impact far beyond our natural borders. I believe there's no better place to start than your home. Home is the space most intimate, most personal. The courage to take stock of our lives, to remember and reflect, to prioritize the time it takes to stop and breathe and gather our memories—all of that creates space for the freedom required to piece ourselves together and show that in our homes.

"Oh, you can't understand!" gasped Katherine. "Things have always been made easy for *you*. You... you seem to live in a little enchanted circle of beauty and romance. 'I wonder what delightful discovery I'll make today'... that seems to be your attitude to life, Anne.... You seemed to have everything I hadn't... charm... friendship... youth. Youth! I never had anything but starved youth. You know nothing about it. You don't know... you haven't the least idea what it is like not to be wanted by any one... any one!"

"Oh, haven't I?" cried Anne. In a few poignant sentences she sketched her childhood before coming to Green Gables.

"I wish I'd known that," said Katherine. "It would have made a difference. To me you seemed one of the favorites of fortune. I've been eating my heart out with envy of you.... I think the real reason I've hated you so is that you always seemed to have some secret delight... as if every day of life was an adventure."

—L. M. Montgomery,
Anne of Windy Poplars

MY STORIED HOME

When our family moved into our old home in 2010, I thought we would never move again. We had bought the quintessential fixer-upper, and we knew it, but it had an amazing yard. The 1919 home had beautiful bones indeed. Excitement was an understatement! I felt up to the challenge, even with our three little ones, who were two years old, one year old, and under one. Little did we know when we moved in that we would soon be expecting number four!

I got right to work before we transported one box, heading over to the new house to paint at night after I put the kids to bed. Within the first few months, a bathtub had nearly come through the ceiling, resulting in an unexpected bathroom renovation, and the heat and air-conditioning units were deemed to be irreparable. Yes, it was a real-life money pit. We lived in part of the house, doing projects incrementally as we saved up money, and slowly, over a decade, the house came to life. Kent and I completed each stage fully believing we would live there forever, and that was the plan until I got an email in late 2019 that changed our course.

Years prior we had gone to a garage sale (hard for me to pass one by), and the kids and I had struck up a conversation with the kind property owner. His plot was so unusual, being close to the river with a few

MINISTERE DE LA SAN
15-22 MAI
1939
SEMAINE NAT
DE L'ENF
COMITÉ NATIONAL de l'ENFANCE 51 AVENUE-

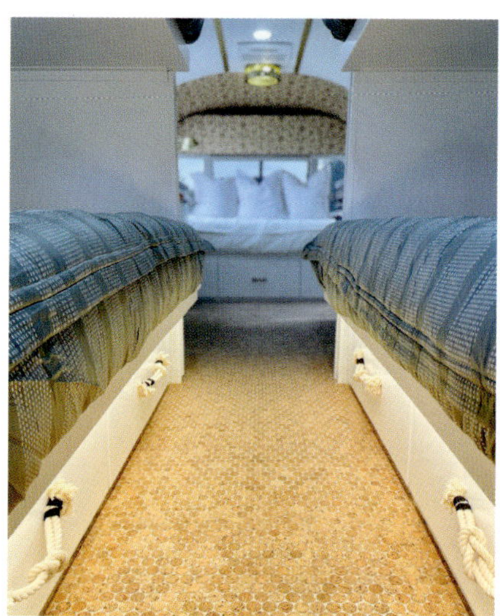

acres yet still close to lots of wonderful amenities—a country-house feel in the city. The kids were running through the woods, loving it, and he said, "You know, if I ever decide to sell this place, I'll contact you." I did not think much of it, brushing the idea aside, telling myself it would never really happen. Until I got an email from the owner stating he had decided to sell.

Moving could not have been further from my mind, but it had been on my husband's. He desired a little more privacy and dreamed of having more land without having to commute. I was more hesitant. The current house on the property was slated for demolition, so we would be building from scratch. As an old-house lover, I never imagined living in a new home. I love creaky floors and jangly doorknobs and wavy glass. While I relished the thought of building a new "old" house, it sounded challenging . . . and expensive. We were not sure we could swing it financially, buying the land and *building* the house. Long story short, after some negotiating, it worked out! The property was ours.

Initially, we planned to stay in our old house while we built the new one, but word spread fast, and soon I was getting calls from around the country. Friends of friends and neighbors who heard we were going to move were interested in purchasing our home and started asking when they could come by. A time was arranged for potential buyers to view it while we took a long walk around the neighborhood. It felt fast and furious—the house sold in a matter of hours in a bidding war. Kent and I were a little shell-shocked for a few weeks after that. Were we really doing this? Were we really selling the home we had lovingly restored all these years, the only home our babies remembered? While emotionally conflicted, we were thrilled and grateful to begin this unexpected chapter, and I threw myself into planning how to make our new-house-that-identifies-as-old dreams come true. But first we had to figure out where we were going to live. Thankfully, the new owners of our old house graciously allowed us to stay a few months while we got the new house started and figured out where we would live in the meantime.

Enter the Airstream. The previous owner of our new property had left his "silver bullet" behind. We figured he would take it with him, but when we got the keys to the property, he said, "You keep it. Turn it into a clubhouse for the kids!" (Which was very generous and meant so much to us.) I laugh now when I think of that sentiment—neither he nor I ever expected it to become our home for two and a half years, but it did. Because we were building during the COVID-19 pandemic, rents were astronomical for what you were getting, and, rather naively, I did not think it would be that long before we moved into the new house. I squinted at that untouched 1969 Airstream sitting in the woods and wondered, *Could we do it?* I knew we would save so much money if we were not renting, plus it sounded like a fabled adventure. I gathered my courage and decided to pitch it to my husband.

His retort back to me will be something of family folklore for years to come. "Ya know, Grace," he said with a long sigh, "I work reeeeeally hard to *not* live in a van down by the river."

But live in a van down by the river we did—two adults, four kids, and two one-hundred-pound Pyredoodles. We found a knowledgeable husband-and-wife team that renovated Airstreams (thank you, Will and Brittany!) and dove right into designing the layout—our queen bed horizontally in one curved end of the trailer; a little desk next to the bed; a five-foot kitchen; two sets of bunks for the kids, complete with a pocket door that locked off our space from theirs; and the sole bathroom at the other curved end. It was loads of fun designing it, almost like putting together a real-life dollhouse. Everything was tiny, and every inch counted—the space would have to accommodate the needs of a family of six in 160 square feet!

The kitchen was small but mighty, and we managed to squeeze in a twenty-inch gas range, a pair of refrigerator drawers (no room for a freezer), a dishwasher drawer, and a microwave. Learning

7th Grade
8th Grade
4th Grade
6th Grade

to cook in a small space like that with little storage required finding items that served many purposes. But, goodness, did I cook in that kitchen! That tiny range cranked out innumerable meals for us, plus two Thanksgiving and Christmas dinners—one for twenty-plus people! (I still laugh when I think about the multiple pans of mashed potatoes I had resting on our bed.) I also learned to cook over fire and gained the survival skills for how to live on a continuous camping trip. There were snakes and bobcats and coyotes. (Oh my! Who knew coyotes were so loud at night?)

And then there was the laundromat. As you can imagine, we were frequent fliers there. But something beautiful came from that too. We ended up having a little community. We helped one another, folding each other's clothes when someone had to step out to get their child from school or practice. I think my children gained some valuable life skills and lessons from this experience. Our laundromat community is an element that I still miss today.

Airstream living definitely was not all fun and games, truth be told—you have to worry about human waste and gray water and black water and running out of propane and the occasional problems winter weather brings. Since I live in Texas, the climate is fairly mild, but a couple of ice storms meant staying in a hotel, which was a nice change. I remember when we went to a hotel for a particularly hard freeze—it had been so long since we lived in a house that we marveled over the size of the seemingly massive thirty-inch kitchen range, how big the closets were, and the amount of drawers we were able to use. There are definitely things you do not realize are nice to have until you don't have them—such as linen closets, which would have been particularly helpful the night all four of the kids woke up projectile vomiting at the same time. (And of course, *of course*, my husband was out of town. Just my luck.) I could not believe my ears and quickly turned on the light, rubbing my eyes to make sure my brain was taking in this scene correctly—the four kids apologizing for not making it to the one toilet, their faces forlorn, damp, pale, sick. It was one of those mom moments you seem to absorb in slow motion, not knowing whether to cry, laugh, scream, or run away. I chose optimistic comedy for this one. "Welp." I shrugged. "It could always be worse." We all chuckled. Let's just say I had to get *real* creative cleaning up that mess! And in everyday life, we definitely had to establish a morning bathroom schedule, as we were all sharing the one tiny loo. To live in close quarters like that, you have to operate as a team—through the good, the bad, and the ugly.

One thing we joke about as a family is that our trailer life enabled one of our kids, who was a little on the messy side in our prior home, to completely transform. Storage in the Airstream was limited, as there were no closets. Everyone had a twenty-by-twenty-inch drawer to fit their whole lives into. It was definitely a good thing I had retail experience and knew how to fold, and now my kids can origami their clothes all sorts of ways. If you struggle with messiness, maybe try tiny living for a while. There's not really a possibility of letting your possessions get too out of order when you live in a space with minuscule storage.

Right before we moved into our house, I asked the kids what they were most excited about. You see, we actually did not allow the kids to go upstairs during the build because of the surprises we had waiting in their rooms. They saw nothing post-framing! As I questioned them about what they were looking forward to, they came up with answers such as "I think I will have a dresser with drawers!" and "I can't wait to have hangers, Mom. That will be so awesome!" and "I cannot believe we will have a washer and dryer *inside* our house!" By the end of our house build, all four of them were impatient and ready to see their spaces, but waiting was well worth it. Showing them their rooms for the first time gave us some of the most precious video footage of my life!

I'll never forget our tiny home in the woods and the life we created there. It was not always trouble-free, but that time was essentially a big reset button for us, the beginning of a new stage of life with older kids. Sleeping with the door open, celebrating Christmases on the deck, making Saturday-morning pancakes on the big outdoor griddle, taking kayak trips in the morning and at dusk, seeing the woods magically come back to life after the winter, being narrowly missed by a gigantic falling tree, and foraging for flowers and leaves to cook with are just a few standout memories. The lessons felt from selling everything, paring down, and living simply affect us even now, a year and a half after we moved into our new old house. The power of finding positivity in what is uncomfortable, practicing gratitude for what is not easy, and uncovering beauty in what is not pretty is a gift to be celebrated.

Since we have only lived in older homes, I am very good at working with what I have—I enjoy figuring out the best plan for wonky layouts, storage problems, or any other conundrums a house poses. When you build from the ground up, these issues do not exist, and, to be honest, that felt a little overwhelming at first. Nearly every option is available when you erect a new home—your boundaries are your lot lines, of course, but style, layout, *everything* is there for the picking.

Our first order of business was to figure out what style of home we wanted. We started with how we wanted the home to feel, so we did not overburden ourselves with possibilities. From the get-go, our overarching vision was to create an "everyday getaway." What if we could live in our vacation home every day? How could we create a home that felt like an exhale and a hug whenever you walked in? That was our goal, and with that dream in mind, plus our story together, we built a home that is ours.

I have a predilection for stone country houses—the kind you find after winding down a long lane, its aged facade and working shutters greeting you. We felt inspired by this type of home, often seen on the Mediterranean side of France. My husband especially loves Texas limestone, and our vision was to use that material and overmortar it to create the aged look we wanted. There were a couple of other styles we tossed around, but we kept coming back to the stone exterior. We also wanted the house to be full of light, to bring the outdoors in as much as possible. This led us to make the house one room deep so the sun streams in every space.

Since we had a direction, it was time to begin our search for an architect. I really wanted someone who was well-versed in designing homes with a true old-house feel. And then I found the renowned Bill Baker. I pored over his books, soaking in all the beautiful details. I was thrilled when he agreed to a meeting. Working with him was such a delight—he is a true master of his craft. He patiently listened to us and kindly tweaked and tweaked again. Kent and I would actually create house models out of LEGOs to play with shape, calculating how many inches of LEGO meant how many feet on our home site. It was really amazing to see our house drawings the first time, to get a 2D idea of what would come to be. We could not be more grateful to Bill for his hand in our home. Getting to collaborate with him was a gift and an honor.

Of course, we needed to find a house builder, and after interviewing several, we settled on Clint Wright, which was one of the best decisions we made in this process. I get to work with lots of amazing contractors and tradesmen, but Clint is special—he understands what needs to be done, but he also has an artistic

eye. He's up for anything and will rack his brain to make something I have dreamed up happen—a trait I greatly appreciate. Clint enjoys crafting spaces that are special, and getting to work with someone whose enthusiasm matches mine has been a joy. After we received the plans from Bill, the city permits, and the materials to start, we were ready to go. I feel like that is flippantly stated, but those bullet points are a whole long process. Once we got through that, we were excited!

Approaching a new build with an old-house story meant creating in a completely different way. I essentially had to write the story of the home as we went along. In our previous old houses, you could look around and see changes that were made in varying eras; you could imagine what decade a wall was opened or a detail added. For our new build, design decisions weaved a narrative throughout. For example, I wanted our entryway to feel like a little old greenhouse—for you to walk through an array of plants in a small space full of windows with lots of light. Nothing too grand. With that in mind, I decided to cover the walls in the same stone as the exterior—eliciting the idea that perhaps, long ago, this had been an open porch. This way of designing, of putting together our home, was really fun. I felt like a kid again, except this time I was embedding my fairy stories into my real life.

During this process, I ruminated on how to authentically place a been-here-forever quality into this home. I did not want to just imitate an old house; I wanted it to *feel* worn and genuine. The answer to this potential problem happened to be in something I love doing: Finding and using vintage and antique materials. Searching the country—especially my beloved Round Top, Texas, which hosts an incomparable antiques fair twice a year—salvage yards around the world via the internet, and my storage unit for one-of-a-kind reclaimed doors, windows, stone, wood, and tile required an immense amount of time, but I loved going on a real treasure hunt. We used "old school" techniques in house building, taking elements of note and re-creating them—laying the floorboards with a gap; using two-by-twelves to create thick, deep walls; making sure the rooms felt cozy and inviting, rather than needlessly large and vacuous. All of these little details, thousands of them, came together to form a picture of an antiquated home with character and a soul. During our build, a frequent comment we got from subcontractors trying to locate the house was that they "could not find the new build—only the old house under renovation." This is the best compliment someone could give!

> All things great are wound up with all things little.
>
> —L. M. Montgomery, *Anne of Green Gables*

When we moved out of our old house, the Airstream was not quite ready yet, so I took the kids on a salvage-yard tour of the southeastern United States. As we trekked the miles, we loaded up our trusty pickup truck with my finds, as much as it could hold . . . and then some. In fact, I stopped in Mississippi to visit our friends Ben and Erin Napier, and Ben actually tattled on me! He sent a photo of our very Clampett-like truck to my husband (who could not come with us because of work) with a note that read, "Just so you know, this is how your wife is driving across the country." Let's just say it's not the first time I've loaded up a truck like that and been a sight to behold! Some of this vintage bounty had a ready slot, while others were simply pieces I loved so I knew there would be a place for them.

As important as it is to have a plan, I have learned no renovation is ever perfectly drafted on a piece of paper. No matter how well you have planned, you have to allow the space to dictate changes when you are standing in it, and be open to that. The tweaks, the changes, the pivots, the what-ifs—this is where the real art happens.

“Home and I are such good friends.”
—L.M. Montgomery, *Anne of the Island*

EXTERIOR

219 Our grass is a special kind of zeon zoysia formulated for North Texas. It's like a meadow grass—we only have to mow it once a year before it freezes. It feels wonderful underfoot, and I enjoy pulling the weeds to feed them to the chickens.
221 A welcoming front porch with antique terracotta tiles pairs beautifully with the over-mortared limestone.
223, 226–227 We are outside people, so having a large back porch to enjoy was a priority. Lots of seating options, a table for meals, and, of course, a swing suited the space we use pretty much year-round. The reclaimed iron columns were painted in stripes for a little bit of fun and as a nod to the Fustic House. (See acknowledgements.)
224 A 250-year-old log cabin became our garage and guest quarters. Using a reclaimed building saved us a ton of money versus building new, plus it has cool factor!
225 A side entry—I especially like the old iron awning we found. We had new glass cut to fit.
228–229 We have never had a pool until this house, and we love it! Brad Kieta of Day VII Pools made all our dreams happen and guided us through our many questions and ideas. My husband and sons do a great job taking care of it, and I am really happy with the mix of stone we did for the surround—marble coping and limestone pavers. I'm especially proud of the backyard as I personally hauled every plant back there in the truck and placed them.
230 The sound of running water is so peaceful. We found this fountain at our favorite local salvage store, Old Home Supply, and installed it on the pathway to the backyard.
231 This iron door was from the house previously on this property. It felt special so we saved it to reuse, lining the back with wood to create a solid door.
232 TOP It was very important to me for our home to have working shutters. We painted them a historically inspired green to tie in with our house's French Mediterranean feel. Antique reclaimed reliefs help give the house a been-there-forever feel.
232 BOTTOM Eating al fresco is nearly a daily occurrence here. This is a “doors open, everyone come over, nothing is too precious, everything can get dirty, it's okay if something gets broken” house.

POSTES

ENTRYWAY

Because of how our home needed to sit on our property, we had a difficult time figuring out how to get the layout we wanted and incorporate a foyer. I did not want to walk into a couch, so we came up with the idea to bump out the front of the house and create an entry with a greenhouse feel. Clad in limestone walls and brimming with plants, it makes you feel as though you're walking through a little garden on the way to the living room. The proportions are just right for an older-feeling home—I think it's really easy to go overly grand in a new build, and I wanted to keep an honest simplicity to the lines and scale.

234 Reclaimed tiles from Antique Floor Company greet you as you open the door.
235 In creating the story of this house, I imagined changes that would have happened through the decades. Perhaps this was originally an open porch that was enclosed, with the vintage Murano chandelier being added in the 1960s. (This is all made up, of course, in the quest to create a new house that truly felt old.)

KITCHEN

Ah, the kitchen, my favorite room to design! I am a big-time cook, so this was a space I dove into with gusto.

237 Our large antique soapstone sink has been amazing—it can handle anything we throw at it, and it continues to look great. And yes, those are the eggs from our chickens! (See pages 338–341.)
238–239 The center of the kitchen is a large worktable that on one side houses our antique soapstone sink, two dishwashers, and a cookie-sheet pullout. On the other side, it contains drawers for dishes and snacks. The cabinet fronts for the dishwashers and the cookie-sheet pullout are made to look like drawers so it appears more like a found furniture piece. I had it built from antique wood and replated some old newels in brass for the corner supports. An old refrigerator door I found in the junkyard for twenty dollars was given new life as our pantry door. I replated the hinges and gave it a fresh coat of paint. People always wonder what's behind it! Reclaimed tile from France lines the back of the range area—blue and yellow are some of our favorite colors. A custom rattan piece was woven to lay over the front of the range wall (it hides the vent insert), but when it arrived, it was a little uneven. I decided its waviness fit the vibe of the house—nothing too pristine here! The tiled end wall of the kitchen houses the refrigerator and freezer, hidden behind large wooden doors salvaged from an old restaurant. These doors were the first thing I bought for the house—their curved handles are so unique. I had pieces of the antique backsplash tile cut to fill the holes where glass used to be. Between the refrigerator and freezer is a pair of larders—one houses baking materials, the mixer, and the blender; the other contains a toaster oven and a coffee-bar area.
240 Spice cabinets were built into each side of the range walls to incorporate unused space; we tiled the doors. (An experiment Clint was up for and made happen!)
241 Underneath the larders are baskets for easy-grab items. One holds baggies, one holds kitchen towels, one holds breads, and one holds root vegetables.

243 I love having a place for the kids to fill up their water bottles, so I designed this water station. The faucet has filtered and chilled water. Long ago, I figured out each kid needs a designated beverage area to avoid a kitchen full of abandoned cups. The oak frame with remnant-stone shelves displays glasses and items we use often.

244 Having a Dutch door in the kitchen has been a dream of mine since I first entered the world of design. Opening the top door is one of the first things I do every morning.

245 You really can't beat the warmth and durability of an antique wood dining table.

246 Any place I can recess storage into a wall, I will use it. This cabinet with glass-front drawers and doors displays some of my more special plates and dishes, along with my napkin and candle collection. I lined the back of the built-in with a piece of Gracie wallpaper I found secondhand online.

247 The conversation starter of the kitchen is our kakelugn, our antique Swedish fireplace. How we love it! I began researching these years ago, and you can find them in all shapes and colors. Kakelugns date back to the eighteenth century, when they were invented because of a shortage of wood in Sweden. After a government mandate to try to find more fuel-efficient solutions, the tiled stove was invented. The kakelugn burned the wood slower and retained the heat for hours. Both my husband and I have quite a bit of Nordic heritage, and after some hardcore searching, I found a kakelugnar and had it shipped over. It was fascinating to watch the assembly—it arrived on a pallet from Sweden in about three hundred labeled pieces. It keeps us nice and toasty on cold days. A unique feature of ours is its warming cupboard for a mug or bowl. An eleven-foot antique dining table from Belgium I found in Round Top has hosted many a meal and art project. In fact, its length allows me to push any craft to the side and still seat my family of six for a meal. I almost always prefer antique dining tables because any patina just makes them better. A nick or a scratch is no problemo!

E T G K

THE HOME UPGRADE

FLOWER ROOM

RIGHT This space is like a butler's pantry, but that never sounds right to me, so we renamed it the Flower Room after the tile that lines the walls. I was inspired by Monet's kitchen in France for this space. I even had the ceiling tiled!

250 TOP These old hand-painted doors were a find from the kids' and my salvage tour. We built our home to be one room deep so you get light from all sides—we want the outdoors all around us. Bringing in something that evokes nature makes the space feel homey.

250 BOTTOM This antique apothecary cabinet was originally one piece. I raised it to create a nice countertop space in this room, custom designing the stone backsplash. Now I can spread out items for parties and prep things I don't necessarily want in full view in the kitchen. I love collecting antique china and glass, and I use them in everyday life. Nothing is too precious to not use daily for us. I want everything to feel touchable and approachable.

251 We use platters daily, but it has always been tricky to store them in such a way that makes them easy to take out. This arched platter rack was designed to match the dimensions of the arched door on the other side of the sink, and now I have a practical solution to the problem of how to efficiently store serving trays.

252 We have a large space for a garden at our home, so I knew this would be the perfect spot to bring in produce and wash it. This breathtaking sink, an original early-1900s creation by Jacob Delafon (now a division of Kohler), was another Round Top find, and I think it is my favorite item in the whole house. A funny thing: When I bought this sink, I had already installed another vintage sink here. But when I rounded a corner and saw this huge, amazing piece of art, I was head over heels. It was more than I ever imagined spending on a sink, but after a little bargaining, it was ours. I have never regretted it. I have a major thing for special old sinks!

253 This is one of my favorite pieces of clothing, a jacket made from a vintage afghan. You can see a color story at play here!

FEUIL. NOYER
RAC. ANGÉLIQUE
BAIES LAURIER
POIVRE CAYEN.

CARLOS MOTA

LIVING ROOM

LEFT The centuries-old fireplace mantel from Pittet Architecturals, accented with antique delft tile; the reclaimed wood floor; and the texture of the lime-plastered walls tell a story of old, while the modern art by the incredible artist Alexandra Valenti balances the space and keeps it fresh.
256 TOP The large antique birdcage houses our ten colorful parakeets, adding to the soundtrack of our home. I love to hear their chirping in the morning while I make breakfast for everyone.
256 BOTTOM A little nook off our living room we call "the snug." It's a cozy spot to play a record and read. I also taped up some antique pressed botanicals I found. It felt good to freely adhere them here and there. Not everything has to be perfectly framed; sometimes the overall look of "Hey, I love this so I put it up" is the easygoing scheme a space needs.
257 The size of our living room was something I went back and forth about. I did not want a giant room; it needed to be big enough to seat a lot of people, but I still desired it to feel cozy and intimate. I'm so happy with how it turned out. I tried to stretch myself in this house stylistically, but I also worked on considering things new to me—like the soundtrack of a house. The fountain's lovely waterfall makes a pleasant melody.
258 An old wooden hook rack is the perfect spot to hang blankets, and I thought it was more interesting to mount it across the window. I always make sure to have one for everyone, and I change them for each season—thicker in the winter and lighter in the warmer months.
259 I took advantage of some extra wall space in the living room to inset some leftover antique beams we had as shelves. The lamp by artist Lewis Trimble and the art from Gillian Bryce were bought at completely separate times, but they jive so well together—proof that what you love often coordinates. Much of the time, we have the steel folding doors all the way open to marry the back porch and living room.

BACK ENTRY

When I married into the Mitchell family, I gained a wonderful extended family—grandparents, cousins, aunts, and uncles—something I never had growing up. Two of our children are named after our beloved Granny and Papa Zack, my husband's paternal grandparents. They live on what we call "the farm" in East Texas. The Mitchells have owned that land for nearly 150 years now, and it holds not only many family stories but many personal memories too. It's where Kent proposed to me, it's where we chop down our Christmas tree every year, it's where our children have jumped on hay bales and made flower crowns. It's special. It seemed only right to honor the family heritage and place we love so much, and that happened to be in our back entry.

260 My husband has spoken with fondness of the fruits and flowers Granny and Papa Z grew on the farm, so I decided to reference those in this space.
262 The hand-painted wallpaper depicts each of these plants, from figs to Granny's gardenias, scuppernongs to muscadines, Papa Zack's pears to peppers, and honors these memories.
263 A view into the back entry from the kitchen. We really do use the dinner bell! It has traveled with us from house to house.

MUDROOM & MUDROOM BATH

RIGHT We all agreed this space should feel happy, so yellow was in order. Papa Zack has passed on now, but when Granny found out we were building a house, she gave us an old door from the original homestead at the farm that burned in the 1850s. There wasn't much that was still usable, but it made for the perfect half door for the entrance to the mudroom.
266 We added a Euro-size washer and dryer in this room for downstairs laundry needs, kitchen towels, and so on. It was a bit of a last-minute decision, but a useful one.
267 The pickwick-pine boards wrap the walls and ceiling, giving the room an aged feel. Everyone has a locker space, drawers were included for catch-all storage, and the dogs each have a bed.
268–269 Because this is a more utilitarian part of the house, I wanted it to feel very undone. Exposed plumbing made from copper pipes, an old wash sink, and a collection of reclaimed tiles I've gathered through the years all came together beautifully. A layering of antique oil landscapes give the walls some softness.

a
beautiful
mess

TEXAS
BOYS STATE

LETTRES
LETTRES
LETTRES
HABITAT
LIVING IN STYLE PARIS
ROBERT STILIN

LIBRARY

LEFT The entrance to the library showcases an unusual antique door. My husband and I are both big readers, as are our children, and we love to collect books. We had an amazing library at our old house, so it was a tall order to design something for our new house that felt as special. In our previous 1919 home, the bookshelves had a neat tongue-and-groove system to hold the shelves in place. I took that idea and expanded the scale for a more modern feel. Now you can really see the slots for the wood, and it made moving the shelves to accommodate various book heights very convenient.

213, 271 A library full of antique books surely requires some oddities, and this peacock seemed to be just the thing. The wallpaper on the ceiling reminded me of the marbled paper found in old books. The large gold-framed art by the prolific illustrator Leonetto Cappiello, a favorite of mine, was a surprise gift from my husband.

272 Inspired by an old movie, I designed this set of doors plus window. The window is in the middle, set behind the antique desk, and the doors on either side go out to a little curved balcony—a nice place to take a book or your laptop. The bookcase to the left of the doors is what we call the Children's Library. You can typically find my girls here snuggled up reading their favorites.

273 Our family piano lives in this room. I love to sit and read while the boys play, fire going, dogs lounging.

-KIMBALL-
CHICAGO

REC ROOM

ABOVE LEFT We had this rattan door and frame woven for the entrance to the rec room.

ABOVE RIGHT Unfortunately, we ran out of the reclaimed basket weave wood floor we used in the rest of the house, but a problem like this is always an avenue to creativity. I sourced old semitrailer flooring, heavily sanded it, and inserted brass dowels where the holes were, cutting them to be even. It ended up having a slight industrial look while still giving the warmth of wood.

RIGHT This space could technically be another bedroom, but for now, we use it as a rec space. It can be a bit of a challenge to make a home workout space pretty, but incorporating vintage finds such as this mirror and the modern 1960s Danish gym ladder help the space feel more lived in, less metal and rubber.

REC BATH

RIGHT Our goal for this room was for it to read like an early-twentieth-century New York YMCA. So imagine my surprise when I found this set of lockers from a true 1920s gym in New York! The classic black-and-white bordered tilescape helps this bathroom feel as though it's been here a long time.

278 A peek into the shower in the rec bath. I included a hand-shower because this is where we wash the dogs. The shower was specifically framed to have no glass. Yes, it stays plenty warm!

279 If you haven't noticed by now, I love old sinks. I had the idea to stripe an old wall-mounted cast-iron sink, but I knew it was something I needed to try out myself first. It works!

M

HALLWAY

RIGHT The groin-vault ceiling was a little tricky to figure out, but the outcome is definitely a wow. Upstairs, we used a wider plank reclaimed wood flooring in various widths. Clint made the antiqued mirror after we had the pieces cut to fit the custom arch.
282 An upstairs hallway showcases a beautiful arched window, a closet with a curved door, a landscape wallpaper, and the secret entrance to my boys' room. Through the wardrobe we go! An antique wall sink is now a drinking fountain for thirsty kids upstairs. There is a chiller and filter system hidden in the closet. Tucked inside the wicker basket is a cup labeled with each person's name.
283 Creating nooks with purpose in a house is a big part of it feeling aged, so I loved designing this reading space at the end of the hallway. I set it apart with a wallpaper surround (even the drawer fronts!), a stack of comfy cushions, an old glass cabinet, and some vintage sconces.

BOYS' ROOM

RIGHT When the boys told me what they were envisioning for their room, I brought them a few wallpaper choices as a jumping-off point. They chose one of the wallpaper options, even flipping it upside down so the dark bottom would now fade into the ceiling they wanted to paint black. I was impressed with their creativity!

286 TOP The big reveal for the boys' room was that behind a closet door was a ladder to a secret room of their own in the attic (shown on page 286 BOTTOM).

287 Entering their space through a wardrobe was an idea my boys threw out one day, and we surprised them with it when they got to see their room. It took some reconfiguring of this old armoire to make it happen, but it really is special.

288–289 The tall wood door with the transom window is originally from an old school, a find from our cross-country salvage trip. "Nosce te ipsum" is Latin for "know thyself," a phrase we talk about as a family. The ability to be honest with yourself about your strengths and your struggles helps you live more empathetically and authentically.

franklin

Ellis
PAC-MAN

nosce

BOYS' BATHROOM

RIGHT The boys wanted a modern feel for their bathroom, but we gave it a little traditional flair so it would not feel separate from the rest of the house. We kept the lines simple but added classic dentil tile trim and reclaimed brick floors to create a cohesive mesh of fresh and salvaged.
292 Details like this vintage "Men" plaque I added to the old schoolhouse door always add interest to a room.
293 Black wood with a cerused grain makes up the furniture-like vanity. I like bathrooms to feel like rooms, to not be too cold, so I warmed up the space with the design of the double sink chest of drawers. Because my boys play the piano, I had the idea for a countertop featuring a piano keys motif. I had a couple of remnant pieces of stone, and the fabricator laminated them together in stripes. Such a statement!

MEN

MEN

GIRLS' ROOM

RIGHT My girls wanted sunshine, sky, and a little pink for their color scheme—a combination of their individual favorite colors. I took the blue-and-white wallpaper three-quarters up the wall around the room, added a picture rail, and painted the rest of the wall and ceiling in the same dusty pink. The chaise has been with me forever, one of my first reupholstery projects from early in my marriage—my husband jokingly calls it "the tongue."

296–297 The big surprise for the girls was that the shoe shelf in their closet is really a secret door that opens up to reveal a small craft/desk area for them to enjoy. We had previously told them it was an "AC room" on the plans.

298 Two big, oft-repeated requests from my girls were for a large window complete with window seat and canopy beds. I honored both asks, of course! The vintage wicker beds are really the stars of the space. A little reading light is nestled in each bed, and the hot-air balloon lights up with a remote—in a variety of colors, no less.

299 Would you believe the canopies did not come with those beds? I found all four vintage wicker pieces of this now combined set at four different times through the years. I wanted to make the canopy bed fantasy come true with items I already had, so when I experimented with how they could be attached and saw it would work, I was beyond excited. (My wonderful Mr. Rick put these together for me.)

dream
&
do

GIRLS' BATHROOM

LEFT AND ABOVE This room ended up being a little larger than we initially planned because of how we expanded our downstairs. But we embraced it with a little step-down area to an open-air shower and soaking tub. An antique window lets in lots of light (I love how it opens!), and each girl picked out the color she wanted for her vintage sink—one blue, one yellow.

302 Like their mama, these little ladies love a bath, complete with a good book, of course. A vintage train rack makes for pretty towel storage.

303 We incorporated this vintage-style toilet because the space was too tight for a standard one, and I added a snazzy wallpaper for some extra pizzazz.

Please

LAUNDRY ROOM

LEFT AND ABOVE This house holds my first true laundry room ever. It's not in the garage or in the basement or in a closet—it's a real room! The Anna Glover textile wallpaper inspired the whole room, floored in a mint-and-brown marble in a classic checker pattern. Of course, I had to include an old sink—a gorgeous lavender cast-iron one with washboards. I've saved this watering can faucet forever, and this was the perfect spot to use it to water upstairs plants!

306 A linen fabric I had on hand became the curtain for under the sink, and the curtain to back the glass of the vintage door. Two very satisfying and quick DIY projects!

307 A pair of salvaged doors from a favorite vendor, East End Salvage, covers the laundry basket and hanging area.

OUR BEDROOM

RIGHT I wanted stepping into our primary suite to feel like entering into another world, a true getaway. Kent likes a dark bedroom, and I prefer a light one, but we compromised on this deep forest limewash paint in our room. It feels slightly moody and beautifully echoes the greens seen out of the massive antique window. The floor-to-ceiling, wall-to-wall window was a Round Top find, and it took quite a bit of plan rearranging to get it to fit, but it makes the whole room. Waking up to this view every day is such a treat!
310 I bought this old set of shutters ages ago and was so excited to see they would fit perfectly behind the bed. Plus we used them as window coverings, really bringing the outdoors in! I enjoy a little topsy-turvy design—using items for a different purpose than their original one. Layering the piece of art over the shutters (do you see the gal peeking above the covers in the painting?) gives the whole look some nice depth.
311 A photographer's backdrop from the 1800s becomes art by attaching the old oil painting—it drapes so lovely over the reclaimed-marble mantel. The vintage low-slung mohair chairs are a good spot for an end-of-day chat.
312 I adore the unexpected of kids' art in tucked-away places. It makes them feel good for their pieces to be out, and it makes me smile to see them.
313 A cozy nook off the bedroom fit our vintage desk just right. I've spent more time here than I thought I would. It's a nice spot to open the window and get some work done.

Ellis

OUR BATHROOM

Tadelakt walls, warm wood, a wallpaper mural, and a copper tub create the "vacay everyday" feel I was hoping for in our bathroom. Tadelakt is a waterproof Moroccan plaster that has been used for hundreds of years.

LEFT AND 316 A jib door is hidden in the hand-painted mural on either side of the tub. One goes to the water closet, and one goes to a linen cabinet.
317 In our previous home's bathroom, Kent and I had an old barbershop sink where we faced each other. It ended up being such a conversation hub for us that I kept the idea in our new bathroom. The double-sided white oak vanity is topped with a heavily veined soapstone and a pair of antique library lamps mounted above. They illuminate the space so beautifully. I like to use as much non-ceiling lighting as I can because it's so much more flattering. An old circular glass window was turned into cabinet doors to face our bathroom storage cabinet. The tadelakt plaster goes right over the drawer fronts, so everything is seamless.
318 A remnant of soapstone became a bench in our shower. I bought this window from the side of the road . . . literally! I especially like to have it open when it's a little chillier outside.
319 An arched bathroom entry felt so dreamy to me, so we made it happen. The bottom of this tile pattern was much too uniform for my taste, so I hand placed the bottom few rows of tile to be more organic. It took me weeks to finish, but it was so worth it! We stuccoed the bottom in black. The "baseboards" are old garden tiles Kent and I found in Round Top. When we saw them, we loved them but could not figure out what to do with them. We walked across the whole field when Kent exclaimed, "We could use them as tiles!" Without a word, I started sprinting back, hoping they would still be there. It was meant to be!

MY CLOSET

RIGHT I had a remnant piece of marble cut to top this vintage table from a department store. It serves as a desk area and a vanity.
322 The glass ceiling was created by spray-painting the backs of twelve-by-twelve pieces of clear glass from the hardware store. The trim, painted a deep olive green, with its recessed design accented by a gold-leaf marker, covers the seams. Simple, readily available items can truly create beautiful details!
323 I have a predilection for drawers, so when I saw this haberdasher's cabinet, I immediately envisioned it as storage in the corner of my closet. The wardrobe doors are upholstered in a green faux leather accented by brass pulls. A botanical wallpaper with wild-looking white flowers (my favorite) lines the walls.

08
POLICE
POLICE

ATTIC

Originally, this space was simply labeled "attic storage" on the plans. But when we were in the framing stage and went up there, the view was so inspiring we knew we had to finish it out. We restructured the ceiling to allow for a large window, and goodness, I'm so glad we did. Mounted above the window and hidden behind the beam is a screen that comes down for movie nights.

LEFT I found a vintage couch online and wrapped it with kantha blankets I bought in stacks at the flea market. They are easy to wash when one takes a spill. I've been a mom long enough to know I'll never be able to keep snacks and drinks out of here!

326–327 The kids picked the wallpaper for this room, even though they were not told where it would go. I love how the stars glow at night. The attic was a surprise for them too! It really does feel like a treehouse up there.

328 Steel, fireproof vintage drawers are designated to each kid for each grade. It definitely helps us keep papers organized! Behind the vintage Moroccan door is where we stash loose Legos.

329 This room has hosted many a sleepover and is a great space for teen hangouts. The built-in bunks have witnessed many a giggle.

STUDIO

LEFT Behind the stone wall, through the old garden gate, is my studio. We built it from leftover materials, and it's such a peaceful spot to create in.
332 Old greenhouse windows, a vintage cast-iron sink, and limestone and plaster walls create a special feeling of discovery, like being in an outbuilding in *The Secret Garden*.
333 If I could, I would live by candlelight. I feel most comfortable in soft, warm lighting. These sconces found on Etsy give off the perfect glow at night. I thought I would paint the plaster, but once I saw the raw color, I liked how it blended with the concrete floor.
334 I'm a wannabe ceramicist so my next step in here is to get a kiln. For now, I have my favorite art books, drawings, and all my samples for my design business stored in here.
335 A plaster piece by a favorite artist of mine, Ron Nicole, graces the sink.
336 I found this stained glass window ages ago at a junkyard, thought it was beautiful, and bought it. It sat patiently waiting all these years, and it seems as if it was meant to be here.
337 The salvaged arched door I used in this space was another item saved from my storage unit, and it inspired the arched ceiling. Anna Glover created this garden-inspired wallpaper for it, and I love it so much.

CHICKEN HOUSE

ABOVE One of my favorite new adventures is being a chicken mom! I'm crazy about them, a real chicken nut. Dottie, pictured front and center in the above left photo (and in the crook of my arm on the cover of this book), is one of my favorites, but he—yes, *he*—greatly surprised us by crowing and turning out to be a rooster. We just couldn't change his name, so Dottie the Roo he will forever be in all his beauty.
RIGHT We built the coop out of scraps, and the kids and I like to sit out here and read a book or just observe the chickens. They have such interesting personalities! I love when they jump up and sit in my lap.
340 There definitely has been some trial and error to this newfound love of chicken keeping, but I'm about two years in now, so things mostly run smoothly.
341 Going out to the coop every morning is something I look forward to. We get eggs in several colors now: olive, sage, wine, dark chocolate brown, pink, and a few different blues. We enjoy sharing them with neighbors and friends, and I'm afraid I will never be able to buy eggs from the store again!

your storied life

"Dear old world," she murmured, "you are very lovely, and I am glad to be alive in you."

—L. M. Montgomery, *Anne of Green Gables*

When envisioning myself writing this book, I pictured putting pen to paper at our house—in the little garden studio. But I quickly discovered it did not feel right. Although it sounds romantic to open the centuries-old garden gate in a stacked-stone wall, to step into the garden and then into a cozy space filled with old wood and warm plaster, to write as I stare out through the wavy-glassed greenhouse windows, my mind and my words did not connect. And there are now twenty-four baby chicks that have taken over my studio and made it look as if a hurricane has hit—but that's a story for another day.

What I have discovered is I need to be near people when I write. For some reason, the words just seem to flow more freely in coffee shops and small cafés—the busier, the better. I'm someone who, to an extent, thrives in chaos (perhaps why I ended up in the world of construction, a field brimming with unpredictable events), so there's something about being surrounded by people, seeing them chat with one another, imagining all their stories—over there's a first date; over here's a new mom; ah, the meeting up of old friends—that reminds me why I am writing a book. My hope is for each person I observe, for each person that lays eyes on this book, to feel seen and important and valued. I suppose the act of simply being near humanity helps me form a connection between these words and reality—what I'm saying makes more sense when I see it all in real time.

Inside all of us is a desire to be known, to matter, to have purpose. A few years ago I was being interviewed, and the host asked me a question I had never been asked before: "I hear you talking about your process, but what has happened in your life that led you here?"

The question elicited a long pause and a flash through my mind. The devastating car accident I mentioned earlier, the one in my early twenties, changed my life. I was hit by an 18-wheeler and pushed the distance of four football fields. The investigators had to calculate the impact twice. They said it didn't make sense—I shouldn't have survived. My parents and three brothers were told to rush to the hospital to say goodbye. But I did survive, though broken in nearly every way possible. I faced death but found life. The preciousness of living, really living, enveloped me, and it was as though a new reality opened up. Despite a slow and painful recovery process, one in which the doctors told me I may never walk again or have children, I grieved, yet held on to hope. And found joy—real joy. Not a fake, saccharine happiness but a joy that comes from walking through deep darkness and coming out alive, not only in body but in spirit.

There's nothing like grief to open the floodgates of anything you have buried emotionally; not only was I dealing with physical pain and the loss of the life I had dreamed of, but I was also unpacking some deep emotional anguish. Gradually, through wise counsel, kind friends, and time, I walked through this pain, rebuilding my physical strength and my soul. Because of how the truck hit me, I ended up with a huge hematoma in my jaw, which took months and months to heal. It was honestly one of the most painful repercussions of my accident. I had a little triangular ruler to measure how much I could open my mouth. My healing progressed inch by inch, or, rather, millimeter by millimeter, and I learned to celebrate every one. As much as the many hours of physical therapy were rebuilding my body, my reasons for being rebuilt metamorphosed too. Life wasn't just about being a good person anymore, being successful, or even being a role model. Something new had stirred within me, and I used it to shape how I respond and listen to others. As a person of faith, I had always felt the purpose of life outside of myself, but the main commandment of "Love God and love others" resonated in my heart and mind with a renewed spirit.

In two other times of my life have I seen similar grief, and in each I emerged with a newfound empathy, a renewed perspective, and a deepened awareness of hope. Recovery like that can infuse someone with a profound sense of strength, and, from that, freedom. Have you ever been around someone who is so comfortable with themselves that it gives you the courage to enjoy that same comfort? That's the beautiful thing about freedom—it's contagious. As much as I wish at times I could go back to that younger me and release her—to talk her through that shyness, that embarrassment, to fix the things that made her want to hide—I can't. But I can remember the old me, and I can share what made her new, and I can model for my children that difference.

You never know how the simple act of seeing other people can change them, and what that might mean to them. Looking people in the eyes, asking your servers their names, inquiring how your checkout person is doing that day—these little things create a habit of seeing people, a trait that can build and spread, reinforcing the fact that we are all in this together. In what can seem like a very lonely world, it is easy to feel overly burdened and, frankly, hopeless. We all struggle with this heaviness, this sense of isolation, and the best way to combat it is through community—family and friends, yes, but also just the people you come into contact with during an ordinary day. A well-lived life is never made up of only grand accomplishments but of small daily acts of love and care, fueled by a mindset of operating in the fabric of life. Sharing stories, sharing lives, sharing hope. You may not be able to change the whole world, but you can definitely change the world you live in. Your actions matter, your smile matters, your words matter. *You matter*, and you are here for a reason.

I write this book with joyful expectation of how these words and ideas will work in your life. Your story is a story that should be told, and the people in your life need you. What better place to start sharing yourself than your own home?

I cannot wait to see it!

"I've had a splendid time," she concluded happily, "and I feel that it marks an epoch in my life. But the best of it all was the coming home."

—L. M. Montgomery, *Anne of Green Gables*

ACKNOWLEDGMENTS

It is not lost on me, as I reflect on each of the photos in this book, that every home renovation is made up of thousands of decisions, the great effort of many minds, hardworking and creative hands, and the trust of homeowners. It's truly a team effort, and I'm so grateful.

To Darren Holdway, who so thoughtfully put this book together with the heart and enthusiasm that would make any author and creator leap for joy, thank you!

To Shannon, who took my call on New Year's Eve, to Kate Macdonald for allowing me to use Anne quotes throughout this book, to Marleene who first shared L. M. Montgomery's books with me, and to Anne Shirley, who forever will live in my mind and heart.

To Jeremy Musson, who kindly lent me his beautiful book on Oliver Messel's Fustic House. I'm mailing it back to you, along with a copy of mine. Many thanks!

To Clint Wright, an exceptional builder and a good man, and his team—with special thanks to Mario Jr., Miza, and Mario Sr.—for bringing our home to life.

To Bill Baker, an architect it was an honor to work with.

To Amy and Hilary, photographing my home with you after all the work and thought that went into it was a dream realized. Thank you!

To everyone who believed in and was involved with "One of a Kind," thank you so much.

To Ty and Charlie, may you always feel the support of the community who loves you.

To Mr. Rick, my favorite Luby's partner, I'll always be your biggest fan.

To Simple Things Furniture in Fort Worth, my favorite home store in the world, and particularly to Jim, Caroline, Patsy, Pam, Misty, and Jonny—thank you so much for all the support and help and encouragement. It has meant so much to me. Jim, your store has been an inspiration of what it means to create a home for decades. That's no easy feat, requiring copious amounts of strategy, artistry, and vision, of which you should be very proud.

To the people dedicated to saving old things in hopes they are given new life, we need you, and thank you.

To Jen Jones, Brian Patrick Flynn, and Jen Woodhouse, who have been there from the beginning, thank you for your friendship.

To Lila, whose wisdom has carried me through, you are a gift.

To Mrs. Hall, the teacher who taught me so distinctively what speaking authentically sounds like and who lives out making others feel seen in such a beautiful way.

To Leanne Ford, whose home was a haven for writing these pages and whose friendship I cherish. You are a kindred spirit indeed.

To my Wednesday girls, you mean so much to me.

To Harper Horizon—Matt, Meaghan, and everyone who supported this book—a deep thank you and big cheers. We did it!

To Bill Stankey, a visionary like no other, I'm so grateful for you.

To Kat, Kelly Kay, Esther, Emily, Meg, Effie, and Julie—each of you has held me up and been the kind of friends I could only dream of. I love you.

To the family that has loved me well, especially my beloved brothers.

To those who have cheered me on, I have felt it, and I thank you—and to those who haven't, you gave me a resilience and a strength I would not have otherwise, and I thank you.

To my Kent, the real writer of the family, who has pored over every word of this book with care and consequently made it much better. Being your wife is the greatest gift of my life.

And to my children, may you write your story with thought and care day by day. I love you, and I like you better than chocolate ice cream.

And thank you, Jesus, for sacrificial love and for a message that overcomes even those who mishandle it.

CREDITS AND SOURCES

GRACE'S NEW HOUSE

(Seen on 1, 3, 4, 95, 213, 219–344)
Architect: William T. Baker | **Builder:** Clint Wright of IEC | **Interior Finishes & Design:** Grace Mitchell | **Photography:** Amy Neunsinger | **Styling:** Hilary Robertson
Items of Note: **2** Fountain from Architect's Daughter in Round Top | **212** Needlepoint by GloryEvelyn Mitchell | **213** Vintage dress from Studio 74 Vintage in Fort Worth; vintage peacock from Susan Apple at Marburger in Round Top | **219** Shutter paint color: Benjamin Moore Southfield Green; working shutters made by Exterior Shutter Company; antique railings and antique stone reliefs from Discount Home Warehouse in Dallas | **223** Tile from Bottega Tile in Fort Worth; salvaged steel columns from Ricca's Architectural Sales in New Orleans | **224** Reclaimed log cabin from Southwest Timber in Fort Worth | **225** Antique glass awning from East End Salvage in Round Top; vintage concrete bench from Looloo Designs in Round Top | **226–27** Vintage outdoor table from Claire Brody Designs; vintage outdoor chairs from Leftover Antiques in Round Top | **228–29** Our dream pool by Brad Kieta at Day VII Pools; striped door from Antiques & Vintage in Round Top | **230** Vintage water fountain from Old Home Supply in Fort Worth | **234** Antique tile floor from Antique Floor Company in France | **237** Vintage soapstone sink from New England Salvage | **238–39** Cabinetry paint color: Devol Bakehouse Green; backsplash tile from Antique Floor Company in France; rattan piece made by Little Jack Horner's; antique fridge and freezer door from Antiquities Warehouse in Arizona | **241** Antique dining table from Rengi Living in Round Top | **244** Counter stools from Rachel Donath | **247** Kakelugn from Lindholm Kakelugnar | **249** Cabinetry and trim paint color: Devol Bond Street Blue; antique sink from Leftover Antiques in Round Top; tile from Bottega Tile in Fort Worth; apothecary cabinet from Antiquities Warehouse in Arizona; antique ladder from Neil Chervin; antique terracotta floor from Pittet Architecturals in Dallas | **250** Antique handpainted doors from Dead People Stuff in Oklahoma City | **254** Lime wash paint color: "Chalet" by Portola; slipcovered sofas from Simple Things Furniture in Fort Worth; pair of vintage chairs from Prize KC in Round Top; antique Delft tile on fireplace from Regis Delft Tiles; antique limestone fireplace mantle from Pittet Architecturals in Dallas; lamp by Holler and Squall in Round Top; metal coffee table from Knock on Wood in Round Top | **258** Vintage hook rack from Big Daddy Antiques | **259** Vintage art from Gillian Bryce Gallery; lamp made by artist Lewis Trimble | **260** Handpainted custom wallpaper made by DeGournay | **265** Yellow paint color: Benjamin Moore Stuart Gold; blue paint color: Sherwin Williams Copen Blue; antique floor tile from Antique Floor Company in France; vintage lights from Chairish | **268** Vintage artwork collected over time from Jardin de France in Round Top; blue toilet from Beautiful Toilet Company | **270** Antique door from Pittet Architecturals in Dallas | **271** Industrial coffee table made by Jonny West via Simple Things Furniture | **272** Marbled ceiling wallpaper from Shoppa by Beata Heuman; reclaimed fireplace mantel from From Europe to You | **273** Antique screen from Pam Krannitz at Marburger in Round Top | **275** Reclaimed semi-truck trailer flooring from Repurposed Materials | **277** Tile from Bottega Tile in Fort Worth | **281** Antique wood floor (throughout house) from Pittet Architecturals in Dallas | **282** Vintage bamboo wardrobe from Pascale Jones in Round Top | **292** Antique schoolhouse door from Architectural Salvage in Tennessee (thank you, Doc!) | **291** Tile from Bottega Tile in Fort Worth | **298** Wallpaper from Farrow & Ball; paint color: Farrow & Ball Calamine; Penguin made by artist Ellis Petty | **300** Vintage colorful sinks from Pasadena Architectural Salvage | **302** Tile from Bottega Tile in Fort Worth | **304** Vintage lavender sink from Kenneth at Gramma's Antique Kitchen; sink curtain from Linen the Label | **307** Antique doors from East End Salvage in Round Top | **309** Linen globe light from Pinch Design | **310** Antique shutter set from Leftover Antiques in Round Top; antique arched windows from Antiquities Warehouse in Arizona | **311** Antique warehouse window from Recycling the Past in Round Top; vintage mohair chairs from Prize KC in Round Top; antique photographer's backdrop from East End Salvage in Round Top; reclaimed fireplace mantel by From Europe to You; vintage rug from Simple Things Furniture in Fort Worth; antique beams from Southwest Timber in Fort Worth | **313** Antique mirror from Box Road in Round Top; lime wash paint color: Ghost Tree from Portola | **316** Handpainted wallpaper by Gracie Studio; Copper cast iron tub from Penhaglion Tubs | **319** Antique garden tiles from East End Salvage in Round Top | **335** Plaster art by Ron

Nicole | **338** Chickens purchased as chicks from Alchemist Farm | **343** Vintage dress from Studio 74 Vintage in Fort Worth | **344** Vintage art from Gillian Bryce Gallery

GRACE'S OLD HOUSE

(Seen on 12–17, 19, 21, 63, 65, 78, 87 (right), 89, 91, 93, 111)
Contractor: Rick & Craig Goodwin | **Interior Finishes & Design:** Grace Mitchell | **Photography:** Robert White (all pages except 66) | **Photography p. 66:** Jennifer Jones | **Styling:** Brian Patrick Flynn & Grace Mitchell | **Shoot Producer:** Brian Patrick Flynn
Items of Note: **12** Chandelier from Old Goode Things | **13** Plaster art by Ron Nicole; wallpaper on stairs and ceiling from Farrow & Ball; paint color: Farrow & Ball Breakfast Room Green | **21** Painting by Kristen Dowd

AIRSTREAM

(Seen on 214, 216)
Contractor: Will Skiles of Trailer Trashin' | **Interior Finishes & Design:** Grace Mitchell | **Photography and Styling p. 214:** Brittany Rhinehart

ROUND TOP PROJECT

(Seen on 23, 25, 103)
Contractor: Samuel Lazcano of Round Top Construction | **Interior Finishes & Design:** Leanne Ford & Grace Mitchell | **Photography:** Reid Rolls | **Styling:** Leanne Ford, Grace Mitchell, and Reid Rolls
Items of Note: **23** Antique table from Architectural Artifacts in Round Top; Aga Classic Electric Range | **25** Vanity and lights from Leftover Antiques in Round Top; marble sink basins from Old World Antieks in Round Top | **103** Vintage brass cabinet from Jersey Junker in Round Top

ARMSTRONG PROJECT

(Seen on 29, 30–35)
Contractor: Rick & Craig Goodwin | **Interior Finishes & Design:** Grace Mitchell | **Photography:** Lisa Petrole | **Styling:** Grace Mitchell
Items of Note: **30–31** wall paint color: Benjamin Moore Chantilly Lace; range and refrigerators from the Big Chill Classic line | **32–33** Dining room paint color: Benjamin Moore Palladian Blue (lacquer) | **34–35** Trim and cabinetry paint color: Benjamin Moore Iced Slate; wallpaper graphic design by Ashley Keane

LEE PROJECT

(Seen on 37–45, 83)
Contractor: Rick & Craig Goodwin | **Interior Finishes & Design:** Grace Mitchell | **Photography:** Lisa Petrole | **Styling:** Grace Mitchell
Items of Note: **37** Entry wallpaper from Serena & Lily; front door and trim paint color: Benjamin Moore Black Forest Green | **38–39** Cabinetry paint color: Sherwin Williams Evergreen; wall and ceiling paint color: Benjamin Moore Simply White; vintage greenhouse lights from Uncommon Lighting in Dallas; range from the Big Chill Classic line | **40–41** Planter basket from Archie's Gardenland in Fort Worth

MCGUIRE PROJECT

(Seen on 47–57, 105)
Contractor: Rick & Craig Goodwin | **Interior Finishes & Design:** Grace Mitchell | **Photography:** Lisa Petrole | **Styling:** Grace Mitchell
Items of Note: **47** Treillage paint color: Benjamin Moore Wedgwood Gray; velvet x-stools from Simple Things Furniture in Fort Worth | **50–51** Cabinetry paint color (custom color matched to tile); tile from Bottega Tile in Fort Worth | **53** Dining chairs from Mainly Baskets Home; stair tile from Bottega Tile in Fort Worth | **54** Door from Old Home Supply in Fort Worth | **55** Custom tile from Restoration Tile; cast-iron sink from Vintage Tub | **56–57** Cabinetry paint color: Benjamin Moore Whipple Blue

MANZKE PROJECT

(Seen on 62, 66, 87 [left])
Contractor: Rick & Craig Goodwin | **Interior Finishes & Design:** Grace Mitchell | **Photography:** Robert White | **Styling:** Grace Mitchell | **Items of Note:** **62** Cabinetry paint color: Benjamin Moore Yellow Green; wall paint color: Benjamin Moore Cotton Balls | **66** Citrus Garden wallpaper by Schumacher | **87 LEFT** Custom stone fabrication by Onis Stone; tub from Vintage Tub

RICE PROJECT

(Seen on 67)
Contractor: Rick & Craig Goodwin | **Interior Finishes & Design:** Grace Mitchell | **Photography:** Robert White | **Styling:** Grace Mitchell
Items of Note: **67** Vintage stall door from Old Home Supply in Fort Worth

FLORES PROJECT

(Seen on 75)
Contractor: Rick & Craig Goodwin | **Interior Finishes & Design:** Grace Mitchell | **Photography:** Lisa Petrole | **Styling:** Grace Mitchell
Items of Note: **70** Graphic design for vintage utensil wallpaper by Kelly Kay Paper; wallpaper printed by Murals Your Way

PRITCHARD PROJECT

(Seen on 71 [Left], 79, 107)
Contractor: Rick & Craig Goodwin | **Interior Finishes & Design:** Grace Mitchell | **Photography:** Lisa Petrole | **Styling:** Grace Mitchell

HOLT PROJECT

(Seen on 71 [right], 75 [top left & bottom right])
Contractor: Rick & Craig Goodwin | **Interior Finishes & Design:** Grace Mitchell | **Photography:** Brian McWeeney | **Styling:** Grace Mitchell

COWDEN PROJECT

(Seen on 74, 101)
Contractor: Rick & Craig Goodwin | **Interior Finishes & Design:** Grace Mitchell | **Photography:** Lisa Petrole | **Styling:** Grace Mitchell
Items of Note: 74 Tablecloth framed by Fort Worth Framers | **101** Tile from Bottega Tile in Fort Worth

THINNES PROJECT

(Seen on 75 [Top Right & Bottom Left])
Contractor: Rick & Craig Goodwin | **Interior Finishes & Design:** Grace Mitchell | **Photography:** Grace Mitchell | **Styling:** Grace Mitchell
Items of Note: 76 Pages from book called *The Parramore Sketches: Scenes and Stories of Early West Texas* by Dock Dilworth Parramore

BROWN PROJECT

(Seen on 82, 86)
Contractor: Rick & Craig Goodwin
Interior Finishes & Design: Grace Mitchell | **Photography:** Lisa Petrole | **Styling:** Grace Mitchell
Items of Note: 82 Cabinetry paint color: Benjamin Moore Kittery Point Green; wall paint color: Benjamin Moore Cotton Balls

KIRCHHOFER PROJECT

(Seen on 70)
Contractor: Rick & Craig Goodwin | **Interior Finishes & Design:** Grace Mitchell | **Photography:** Robert White | **Styling:** Grace Mitchell
Items of Note: 70 Wall and ceiling paint color: Farrow & Ball Hague Blue

RIOS PROJECT

(Seen on 109)
Contractor: Rick & Craig Goodwin | **Interior Finishes & Design:** Grace Mitchell | **Photography:** Lisa Petrole | **Styling:** Grace Mitchell

FINDLEY PROJECT

(Seen on 113, 130–41)
Contractor: Rick & Craig Goodwin | **Interior Finishes & Design:** Grace Mitchell | **Photography:** Lisa Petrole | **Styling:** Grace Mitchell
Items of Note: 113 Stationery pad paper from Kelly Kay Paper | **131** "Hope" sign made by Mello Signs in Fort Worth | **136** Window from Discount Home Warehouse in Dallas; cast-iron sink from Vintage Tub; tile from Bottega Tile in Fort Worth | **137** Vintage steel fridge cabinet from Old Home Supply in Fort Worth; cabinetry paint color: Benjamin Moore Van Heusen Blue | **138–39** Island lights from Olde Goode Things | **141** Striped sisal wallpaper from Schumacher

NOKES PROJECT

(Seen on 118–27)
Contractor: Rick & Craig Goodwin | **Interior Finishes & Design:** Grace Mitchell | **Photography:** Lisa Petrole | **Styling:** Grace Mitchell
Items of Note: 118–19 Exterior paint color: Benjamin Moore Soot | **120** Mural photography by Lisa Petrole, mural by Murals Your Way | **122–23** Kitchen backsplash is vintage basketball court flooring from Repurposed Materials | **124** Cabinetry color: custom blue stain

SCHULZ PROJECT

(Seen on 144–55)
Contractor: Rick & Craig Goodwin | **Interior Finishes & Design:** Grace Mitchell | **Photography:** Lisa Petrole | **Styling:** Grace Mitchell
Items of Note: 144 Entry trim paint color: Benjamin Moore Oasis Blue; wall paint color: Sherwin Williams Shell White | **145–47** Custom wallpaper by Murals Your Way; graphic design for wallpaper by Ashley Keane | **150–51** Tile from Bottega Tile in Fort Worth; custom made metal backsplash sign by Mello Signs in Fort Worth | **153** Photography for cabinet wallpaper by Charlie Schulz; cabinet wallpaper from Murals Your Way

HUNT PROJECT

(Seen on 158–67)
Contractor: Rick & Craig Goodwin | **Interior Finishes & Design:** Grace Mitchell | **Photography:** Lisa Petrole | **Styling:** Grace Mitchell

HORCHNER PROJECT

(Seen on: 170–83)
Interior Finishes & Design: Grace Mitchell | **Photography:** Lisa Petrole | **Styling:** Grace Mitchell
Items of Note: 170–71 Beams sourced from Southwest Timber in Fort Worth; backsplash tile from Bottega Tile in Fort Worth | **172** Kitchen island paint color: Farrow & Ball Bancha | **175** Trim and ceiling paint color: Sherwin Williams Stardew; furniture from Simple Things Furniture in Fort Worth | **178** Bedroom paint color: Sherwin Williams Rainwashed; wallpaper by Sandberg "Pine" in Gray | **183** Custom printed photo tile by Mello Signs; exterior paint color: Benjamin Moore Black Forest Green

ABRAHAM PROJECT

(Seen on 186–95)
Interior Finishes & Design: Grace Mitchell | **Photography:** Lisa Petrole| **Styling:** Grace Mitchell
Items of Note: 188 Tile from Bottega Tile in Fort Worth | **192** Bedroom paint color: Benjamin Moore Silver Cloud | **195** Wallpaper by Muriva "Dogs in Frames"

MAYO PROJECT

(Seen on 198–209)
Interior Finishes & Design: Grace Mitchell | **Photography:** Lisa Petrole | **Styling:** Grace Mitchell
Items of Note: 199 Living room paint color: Benjamin Moore Spring Mint | **200** Craft organizing by Jennifer Jones | **201** Wallpaper is Lulie Wallace "Suzanna" | **202** Cabinetry paint color: Benjamin Moore Buxton Blue | **206** Custom murphy bed made by Jen Woodhouse

ABOUT THE AUTHOR

Grace Mitchell loves illustrating the lives of her clients through home design. Her unique way of creating spaces has garnered national attention, particularly through her television series, *One of a Kind*, on HGTV. Grace has starred in several design television series and has appeared on the Food Network. Her work has been showcased in *House Beautiful*, *The Los Angeles Times*, *Country Living*, *Better Homes & Gardens*, *HGTV Magazine*, and in media outlets *Domino*, *Southern Living*, *Elle Decor*, *People*, *The Boston Globe*, and more. Treasure hunting at flea markets (especially Round Top in central Texas) and antique stores, being outdoors, antique books, all things home, and creating anything from food to pottery are Grace's passions. She is grateful every day for her beloved family—her husband, Kent, and four growing kids—and their lively home in Fort Worth, Texas, the base of operations for her design firm. Follow Grace's projects and adventures on Instagram, @astoriedstyle, and her website, www.astoriedstyle.com.

"I don't want sunbursts and marble halls. I just want *you*."

L. M. Montgomery, Anne of the Island